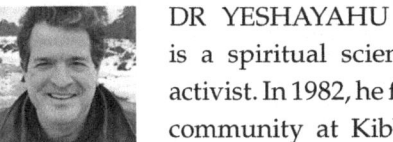

DR YESHAYAHU
is a spiritual scien
activist. In 1982, he fc
community at Kibb
2009, he has headed the Global School of
Spiritual Science. At the centre of his research is the development
of human consciousness in philosophy, history, art, natural
sciences and social life. He is the author of *Cognitive Yoga, The
Three Meetings, Jerusalem, The Twilight and Resurrection of
Humanity, Spiritual Science in the Twenty-First Century, The Event
in Science, History, Philosophy & Art, The New Experience of the
Supersensible, The Modern Christ Experience and the Knowledge
Drama of the Second Coming, Volumes 1-4, America's Global
Responsibility, Cognitive Yoga: How a Book is Born,* and his most
recent work, *The Time is at Hand!*

THE SPIRITUAL EVENT OF THE TWENTIETH CENTURY

An Imagination

The Occult Significance of the 12 Years from 1933 to 1945 in the Light of Spiritual Science

Yeshayahu (Jesaiah) Ben-Aharon

TEMPLE LODGE

Temple Lodge Publishing,
Hillside House, The Square,
Forest Row, RH18 SES

www.templelodge.com

First edition 1993
Second edition 1996
Third edition 2025

A catalogue record for this book is available from the British Library

ISBN 978 1 915776 30 3

Cover by Morgan Creative incorporating 'Das Faust-Motiv mit inspiri-
erendem Genius' (from Rudolf Steiner's first Goetheanum building)
Typeset by Symbiosys Technologies, Visakhapatnam, India
Printed by 4Edge Ltd., Essex

There we are already [at the end of the twentieth century] after the 'appearance of the Sun' that has to take place in etheric Imagination for earthly life. The Christ will appear for the Earth when almost everyone has abandoned Him; when all that mankind knows of Him is His name.[1]

---

[1] Helmuth von Moltke through Rudolf Steiner, in *Helmuth von Moltke 1848-1916, Dokumente zu seinem Wirken*, letter 74 to Eliza von Moltke, 27 March 1919 (Perseus Verlag, Basel 1993).

Contents

Note on the Third Edition

When I review my first book more than thirty years after its first edition was published in 1993, I have the feeling that the Imagination of the Spiritual Event of the Twentieth Century, described in the third chapter, should not be changed. This Event stands today before my inner eye as it stood then. The original formulation and formation, that summarized 15 years of research, has its own unique consistency. Only the notes, preface, introduction and the auxiliary chapters had to be updated, out of the signs of the present time.

In my following books this research was augmented and expanded: *Cognitive Yoga: Making yourself a new etheric body and individuality* (2016), *Spiritual Science in the Twenty-first Century: Transforming Evil, Meeting the Other, and Awakening to the Global Initiation of Humanity* (2017), *The Twilight and Resurrection of Humanity: the history of the Michaelic movement since the death of Rudolf Steiner, An esoteric study* (2020), *The Three Meetings: Christ, Michael and Anthroposophia* (2022), *The Time is at Hand! Ahrimanic and Michaelic immortality and the apocalypse of the age of Michael* (2024), *The Modern Christ Experience and the Knowledge Drama of the Second Coming* (2024).

Yeshayahu (Jesaiah) Ben-Aharon
Tel Aviv, Israel, Easter 2024

Preface

The cosmic-earthly timing of Rudolf Steiner's last earthly life was such that he could have reached his seventy-second birthday in the most decisive year of the twentieth century, namely, 1933 (1861-1933).[2] This means that he could have, first, completed his just begun tenth seven-year life period, from the age of 63 to 70 during the years 1924-31, bringing the Christmas Foundation Conference impulse, the School for Spiritual Science and the new social formation of the General Anthroposophical Society to their maturity on the Earth. And then, having lived that long, he could have been granted the allotted full cosmic time measure of earthly human life to develop Anthroposophy further in his next two years of life, (70-72) from 1931 to 1933, and so complete the anthroposophical bridge for humanity from the beginning of the new age of light to the moment in which, on the one hand, the apocalyptic beast was set free from its captivity in the Earth and, on the other, the Etheric Christ began to be perceived by the new, natural supersensible faculties (see Chapter 2).

In this way he could have brought his life task to its destined fulfilment: to create for humanity as a whole, in and through the Anthroposophical Society, *the fully conscious*, unbroken and continuous, bridge across the abyss of the threshold that broke into ordinary human consciousness in the twelve years 1933-45 from the *unconscious* crossing process of the threshold that had already begun for humanity as a whole in the middle of the *nineteenth century*. Anthroposophical spiritual science, as a living spiritual, cultural and human-social reality, could have then penetrated and transformed the highest and lowest forces of the threshold at the very historical moment in which they approached humanity, from 1933 onward, and made them available as healing,

---

[2] This is described in greater detail in the third lecture of my book, *The Twilight and Resurrection of Humanity—The History of the Michaelic Movement since the Death of Rudolf Steiner, an Esoteric Study* (Temple Lodge 2020), entitled: 'The being of Rudolf Steiner'.

strengthening and uplifting forces for the Michael age, the fifth post-Atlantean epoch and the new cosmic age of light as a whole.

The world tragedies of the second third of the twentieth century, and especially of those twelve years, came about because Rudolf Steiner could not bring his life-task to its completion. This was not his failure but *our own*. This failure has constituted, since then, the main anthroposophical karmic debt of the last century, and this applies not only to the individuals who were *physically* involved in the anthroposophical life of the first and second thirds of that century but to all the members of the Michael School that strive truly to make the carrying and resolving of this karmic debt into their own karmic duty. Now as long as, and to the extent that, this debt remains unconscious and its carrying is not taken as a central anthroposophical duty of true self-knowledge *in the present time*, its unredeemed forces for all future to come will work in such a way that they make the time-picture of the twentieth century as a whole—and its deeper anthroposophical significance—obscure and opaque. This is the reason why the dedication and loyalty to this unrealized life-time potentiality and possibility, inherent in Rudolf Steiner's unfinished life-task, is a real occult condition for the ability to develop the anthroposophical forces needed for finding a connection to the accomplishment of the great tasks of the end of the last century—which, although on Earth unnoticed by most people, was nevertheless perceived in the spiritual world, as I have borne witness to in *The Twilight and Resurrection of Humanity* and will indicate further below—and that we can develop the necessary Michaelic forces for the great tasks that lie ahead of us now at the beginning of the present century. Only if we follow the inner call of this occult Michaelic duty can we come to a vitally important understanding concerning the anthroposophical tasks of the last seven-year period of the twentieth century, our present time, and beyond.

We can come to realize that until now we could only observe and study *the negative physical* results of the fact that Rudolf Steiner's earthly life came to a too early end. After Rudolf Steiner's death, the future, redeeming life-and-time stream of the age of Michael and the new age of light could not work in a conscious way into the physical world. Because of this, those forces of hindrance, that brought about Rudolf Steiner's premature death in the first third, came to an outward victory in the events of the twelve years 1933-45, both in the Anthroposophical Society and the world at large. But if we take upon ourselves consciously the karma created by those forces that hindered the development of the full potentiality of the life-body of Rudolf Steiner at the beginning of the last century, it opens to us unknown aspects of the time-secrets of the twentieth century. Such an overcoming of the life-and-time hindering forces brings us—then as well as today—into the *true* life-and-time stream of the twentieth century; it discloses the living spiritual moment of the last seven years of the last century and shows that its innermost core consists in its capacity to become for us a conscious summation and extract of the life-and-time body of the twentieth century as a whole. It may allow us to look backwards into that last century's supersensible stream of life-time and add, to the *physical* historical view of this, the *supersensible* development of the Michael stream at the same time.

Then we can realize that the negative results of our failure in the first third of the century also created the possibility for a transformation of this failure into a higher good in the supersensible anthroposophical life in the second third of the century. The spiritual-scientific research presented below shows that, beside the externally visible historical tragedies of the twentieth century caused by Rudolf Steiner's unfinished life-task, there also occurred *the hidden, purely supersensible compensatory Michaelic act* that, on a higher level, aimed to compensate for this omission. And this realization is gained if we are able to use now, on the Earth, those unfinished anthroposophical life-forces of Rudolf Steiner's unfinished life-task, *in order to investigate also the supersensible, hidden Michael-Christ Event of these crucial transforming years for the world and humanity.*

The Spiritual Event of the Twentieth century, described below, in which the greatly reduced Michael stream took part, created in the years of these world catastrophes—through a purely supersensible action—the bridge over the abyss of the century, which had to be established *physically* by 1933, but whose building process was prevented. It is now our task to create this bridge consciously and physically on the Earth, working from the other side of the century's abyss backwards towards its supersensible centre, and forwards towards the incoming Michaelic stream of the twenty-first century, in which are found the needed *future* forces for the physical task of the Michael stream on the Earth in the twenty-first century. The formative Michaelic life-forces that directed and shaped this supersensible Michaelic Event were, and are, the same life-forces by means of which we could awaken to the reality of this Event and raise it to full consciousness in the last seven remaining years of the twentieth century. *These are those forces that have constituted, since the laying of the Foundation Stone of the General Anthroposophical Society in the Christmas Foundation Conference of 1923/4, the still fresh and vibrant, unused forces of the tenth seven-year period in the life-task of Rudolf Steiner, 1924-31, and the two more years of his originally possible earthly life-time, 1931-33.* The fully conscious, inwardly dedicated loyalty to these forces is the indispensable anthroposophical foundation that could alone guarantee the *occult continuation and inner unity*, of the beginning and end of the Michaelic work in the last century, as well as its rebirth in the present century. This inner, spiritual continuity and unity of the beginning and end of this century was achieved to the extent that true Michaelites were able to bring to full spiritual-scientific consciousness the purely spiritual Event of the *middle* third of the twentieth century. This event took such a form in the middle third precisely because its essence was not realized on the Earth in the first third of the century, as was intended, under entirely different conditions and in other forms.

This also meant that, in a manner which may appear paradoxical to our common understanding of time, the seven years (plus two), from 1924 to 1931/3 that seemed lost entirely for the anthroposophical task in the last century, could still be made use of, in a spiritualized and metamorphosed form, in the last seven years (plus two) of 1993-2000/2. And even today it still applies: if we *do* make this reversed time-way and spiritually actualize the unfinished but possible bridge-way that was to lead consciously to the twelve years 1933-45, *we find ourselves inside the supersensible process of this central Michael-Christ Event of the Twentieth Century.* We become active participators in the action and sacrifice of the Michael School, which made possible the culmination of the second Mystery of Golgotha for our age.

This was—and still is, therefore—an important aspect of the threefold time secret of the twentieth century: first, the possible life-forces of the years 1924-31/3 that had to be used *physically* on the Earth but were not, and so remained potential and future orientated. Second, the *purely supersensible* use of these forces in the century's Event. And then, thirdly, the possibility—which was finally realized after all—to actualize these forces at the end of the century, physically on the Earth, and *at the same time* also grasp their true supersensible nature. So that what was not yet possible in the years 1924-33, and was then made separately possible in the century's Event of the twelve years, but then only purely supersensibly, could be realized now in its totality—as a seed that has begun to germinate in our twenty-first century for all time to come—uniting the physical and spiritual time-streams of our century together in and through each other, at the same supersensible *and* earthly time.

This gives us the following picture of the three parts of the twentieth century from the point of view of the present:

1) *First third*—Hindered life-forces that were destined for earthly-anthroposophical work until 1933; forces that were destined for realization on the *Earth* were *spiritually* preserved.

2) *Second third*—The unused life-forces that remained spiritual become *purely supersensible*, anthroposophical formative forces, shaping the purely spiritual-supersensible Michael Event of the century.

3) *Last third*—The physical-earthly use of the preserved and, until now not fully used, potential earthly forces of the first third, together with the pure, spiritually active anthroposophical life-forces of the second third. This leads to a fully conscious and earthly realization at the end of the *last* third of the unused forces from the end of the *first* third, through the comprehension of the purely supersensible Event of the *second* third.

This synthesis of the first and second thirds of the twentieth century in its last third will still be able to bring, in this present century, the most significant physical achievements and developments of a reborn Anthroposophy in the physical world together with its hidden, supersensible achievements and developments in the spiritual worlds. The union of these two parallel anthroposophical streams enabled the true—although unnoticed by most people—culmination of Anthroposophy in our time, and also provided the right foundation for its rebirth and recreation at the beginning of the twenty-first century. It is a culmination that, however, has to be realized and achieved by all those who wish to take part in its present and in its future potential.

The always preserved and living possibility to bring *the whole* spiritual development of the Michael stream in the twentieth century, in its physical as well as in its spiritual aspects, to a fully conscious new anthroposophical *earthly as well as supersensible* life at its end, could be found in the eternal Life Spirit forces of Anthroposophy. This Life Spirit constitutes the substance of the Christmas Foundation Conference and is the Foundation Stone of the School for Spiritual Science and the General Anthroposophical Society, initiated and consecrated by the life-sacrifice of Rudolf Steiner: 'This is the *Michaelic Grail* that descended to Earth at the Christmas Conference of 1923-24 ...'[3] With its help alone could the integration of the physical and supersensible anthroposophical life-streams of the twentieth century into *one* conscious stream be achieved.

---

[3] S.O. Prokofieff, *Rudolf Steiner and the Founding of the New Mysteries* (Temple Lodge Publishing, 1994).

The Foundation Stone, if taken in *this* sense, can become the power that moulds inwardly the organs of a specifically spiritual-scientific imaginative faculty, which can grasp the Michael-Christ Event of the Twentieth Century.

As in the case of the *regular* karma and reincarnation laws of a human individuality, so it is also in the *exceptional* case of the karma and reincarnation of the soul and spirit individuality of the being of Anthroposophia in the twentieth and twenty-first century: it is the Life Spirit that metamorphoses and transmits the spiritual harvest and karma of the previous earthly life into the next: 'Just as the Life Body reproduces the form of a species from generation to generation, the Life Spirit reproduces the soul from one personal existence to the next.'[4] This Life Spirit, which bears the supersensible form and substance of the Christmas Foundation Conference and the anthroposophical Foundation Stone, is the power that shaped the *planetary* Midnight Hour event of the Michael School in the middle third of the twentieth century, and carries it into its present reincarnation on the Earth. It carries, therefore, the secret of its occult continuation and rebirth in the Michael age. In this planetary Midnight Hour of the Michael School the 'human being of Anthroposophia' went through Her greatest probation and metamorphoses, through which the spirit harvest and karmic fruit of the first third of that century was transformed and reborn spiritually again for its renewed life-task in the present century.

Two significant indications that were given by Rudolf Steiner concerning his supersensible task after his death must be mentioned here. The first is found in Ita Wegman's notes for a lecture held in London on the 27 February 1933: 'Blossoming during the Christmas Conference. Renewal of Anthrop. Society. After a high point reached, why not a continuation? Said all that could be taken up by people. Now emphasis on spiritual world. The dead must be prepared for new Earth incarnation as also 3rd hierarchy.

---

[4] R. Steiner, *Theosophy* (GA 9).

Here a great mystery!'[5] The second was given to Johanna Grä-
fin von Keyserlingk on the morning of the cremation of Rudolf
Steiner's physical body: 'I shall return and reveal the Mysteries when I shall have succeeded in founding an altar in spiritual
worlds, a place of worship for human souls. Then I shall return.
Then I shall continue to reveal the Mysteries.'[6]

The imagination of the Spiritual Event of the Twentieth Century presented below describes the actual supersensible action of
the Michael School in the middle third of this century, through
which this *place of worship* and its *altar* were founded in the etheric world of the Earthly-Human Sun.

The fulfilment of the anthroposophical karmic debt and duty
of the first third of the century through the practice of the living spirit-recollection, spirit-mindfulness and spirit-vision of the
Christmas Foundation Conference impulse in these last seven
years of the twentieth century can become the power that will
also enable the conscious Michaelic spirit-recollection, spirit-mindfulness and spirit-vision of the Spiritual Event of the
Twentieth Century, in which the living heart-centre and life-
blood of the evolving Time Spirit and the being of Anthroposophia in this century and in the Michael age as a whole are found.

---

[5] J.W. Zeylmans van Emmichoven, *Wer war Ita Wegman*, Vol. 1, Heidel-
berg 1992, p. 292.
[6] Count Adalbert von Keyserlingk, *Koberwitz 1924-Geburtsstunde einer
neuen Landwirtschaft*, Niefern-Öschelbronn, 2nd ed. 1985, p. 178.

Introduction

This short study of the Imagination of the twentieth century's central spiritual Event is the outcome of lectures I gave on the subject to members of the Anthroposophical Society in Germany and Great Britain in the years 1992-93. The subject of the Imagination was intended as the last chapter of my book *The New Experience of the Supersensible* (Temple Lodge, 1995).[7] After describing in detail the spiritual-scientific investigation of the modern Christ experience, this work should have ended with an imaginative 'time picture' of the twentieth century as a whole and its supersensible culmination at the end of the century. This culmination, whose light increasingly illuminates the whole last third of the twentieth century and reaches a dramatic climax at its end and at the beginning of the next, also contains the seed for the Michaelic task of the twenty-first century. It was in the course of researching the 'time picture' of the twentieth century as a whole that my attention was increasingly led to concentrate on the beginning of the second third of that century, especially on the 12 years 1933-45.

However, when writing the above-mentioned book I was not yet able to describe this period of time in concrete detail. The Imagination itself had been, indeed, quite clearly present before my inner eye for some years, but only by speaking on this theme to anthroposophical audiences did I find the words and the mental pictures needed to portray it adequately. The lecture tours in Germany and Great Britain were especially significant for me in this respect. During these lectures I could strongly feel how the guiding hand of the Time Spirit, Michael, was active through the higher beings of the listeners, enabling me to grasp, with exact thinking, the supersensible mysteries of the aforementioned

---

[7] Now published as extended new edition as *The Modern Christ Experience and the Knowledge Drama of the Second Coming*, 4 Vol., Independently published, 2024.

12 years. I increasingly perceived how, the more I entered deeper into these mysteries and gained in courage, the more the higher selves of the listeners were active and creative in offering the required thought-forms out of their own beings. And though the listeners were not conscious of this—paradoxically, many of them would later resist it in their ordinary consciousness—the more this mutual spiritual dialogue and co-operation with the higher spiritual being of the audience developed, the clearer and surer was the guiding hand of the Time Spirit felt.

In this way, a united group effort revealed itself, active from both sides of the threshold, in which the speaker becomes the organ for expressing the mysteries of the Michaelic Christ impulse that wishes to manifest at the present time. He becomes the hearer who listens most attentively to the spiritual Word of Michael, describing the mysteries of the Spiritual Event of the twentieth century. He then transforms his listening-being so that he is able to express what is living and weaving through the spiritual hearts of the audience. There takes place a mutually quickening and awakening supersensible-sensible dialogue that raises and enhances the faculties of the speaker (the real listener) and listener (the real speaker) at the same time. Through this experience, man gains the conviction that the secrets of the new Revelation of Christ in the present age, in so far as they are grasped through the guidance of Michael, can only articulate themselves through a suitable *community language* which must be consciously created in our time.

A mutual human and spiritual awakening on all levels of life today becomes essential when we wish to find the power needed to penetrate with full consciousness and to speak about the deepest riddles of the twentieth and twenty-first centuries. Only a true Michaelic community spirit can help us, for alone we can achieve very little in this respect. This is an absolute necessity when we wish to raise the Imagination of the twentieth century's Event, and its continuation into the twenty-first century, to full consciousness.

In and through the Christ Event of our time, the deepest human and Michaelic forces are working, continuously shaping our destiny. They spring from the very heart centre of our Time Spirit. The self-consciously formed vessel of true Michaelic community is the only means to grasp them, make them comprehensible and then actually realize them daily, in the social life of humanity, now, in this present century.

1

Anthroposophy as the Living Language
of the Present

The Spiritual Event of the twentieth century, described in this book, could be grasped consciously on Earth since the 70s and 80s of the last century, and it guides the development of the new Michaelic movement and school until the centenary of the beginning of the Second Coming and the Spiritual Event of the twentieth century in this century, in 1933-45, 2033-45. It may also be considered as belonging to the whole time span of the twentieth century, which is the first century of the new age of light begun in 1899. In order to become the living language of the present, modern spiritual science must learn to speak directly out of the deeper supersensible events of our time as a whole. In the context here, this means the investigation of the occult significance of the Imagination of the century's spiritual Event which took place behind the curtain of the world catastrophes of the years 1933-45, and continues in ever new transformations. However, before studying this Event, we should explain, at least in outline, our spiritual-scientific method in investigating the greatest occult riddle of our time.

In my book, *The New Experience of the Supersensible*, I called this method 'the knowledge drama of the Second Coming'.[8] It is based on the fact that, since the beginning of the Michael age in 1879, and the end of the small dark age, Kali Yuga in 1899, two central spiritual influences stream increasingly into the consciousness of man. The first is the Michael power, which guarantees the new human faculty of pure, living thinking and individual experience of freedom, and the second is the new supersensible perception that could enable man to perceive the appearance of the Christ in the etheric realm since 1933. Now the Michael and

---

[8] The new edition is entitled *The Modern Christ Experience and the Knowledge Drama of the Second Coming*. See fn 7.

Christ streams have to be integrated through the development of modern spiritual science. The whole of Anthroposophy, as Rudolf Steiner conceived and actualized it, is the result of this integration. And out of the different spiritual-scientific ways to achieve this integration we shall emphasize here one that begins with the spiritual path based on *The Philosophy of Freedom*.[9]

This path aims to transform thinking into an active, willed, creative spiritual force, and to penetrate the active will with the clarity and stability of thinking. That is to say, to cross thinking

---

[9] The title *The Philosophy of Freedom* is used here in a broader sense to denote the whole of Rudolf Steiner's philosophical-anthroposophical life-work. The main stations on the way are as follows.

First are three philosophical works: *A Theory of Knowledge Implicit in Goethe's World Conception* (1886, GA 2); *Truth and Knowledge* (1892, GA 3); and *The Philosophy of Freedom* (1894, GA 4). These must be studied together with the introductions and comments to Goethe's natural-scientific writings, *Goethean Science* (1883-97, GA 1 a-e).

Second are some lectures of 1908 (14 and 20 March, 20 and 28 October, 8 and 13 November, in GA 108), and the article 'Philosophy and Anthroposophy' (GA 35). These mark a step forward in bringing together philosophy and Anthroposophy.

Third is the last chapter of *The Riddles of Philosophy* (1914, GA 18), entitled 'A Brief Outline of Anthroposophy', and with it the linking of this theme to the problems of modern natural science in *The Riddle of Man* (1916, GA 20), and modern philosophy and psychology (in connection with Brentano) in *The Riddles of the Soul* (1917, GA 21), in which also the first and fundamental relation is established to the threefold picture of man and the problems of the 12 senses.

Fourth, one should mention the whole series of the School of Spiritual Science lecture cycles, beginning in 1920 with the new linking of philosophy, Anthroposophy and Goetheanism in *The Boundaries of Natural Science* (GA 322) up to the last course given in December 1922 and January 1923, *The Origins of Natural Science* (GA 326). The whole was then crowned in the letters to the members in *Anthroposophical Leading Thoughts* of 1924/5 (GA 26).

All in all, Rudolf Steiner's work in the field of the theory of knowledge and the philosophy of science and its relation to Anthroposophy was his life's work, extending over more than 40 years.

and will in and through each other, so that thinking will be thoroughly willed and the will thoroughly thought.[10] What is normally polarized is thereby reversed: inside-out for the will, outside-in for thinking. The hidden will element in thinking is spiritualized and becomes the active formative force of cosmic thinking; the hidden thought of the will is condensed and becomes the centre of the creative will, active in the spiritual foundation of the physical world and body. 'Freedom' is the result of the first, 'love' the result of the second transformation.[11] And when the two results are also crossed and their essences are mutually exchanged, the cognitive and moral foundation is formed for human life in the present and future stage of human evolution.

Through the love of freedom and the freedom of love, the consciousness soul—the soul flower and spirit-seed of modern man—grows healthily, matures and provides nourishing, life-giving cultural and social fruits. It also provides the best soil for the flourishing of spiritual science and its development in the human soul.[12]

That malady from which Anthroposophy has been suffering most since its inauguration in the beginning of the twentieth century, is prevented only in this way. For Rudolf Steiner, Anthroposophy was, is, and shall be the living and creative expression of the human being in his wholeness, uniting in a free manner

---

[10] See the lecture of 6 February 1923 in *Awakening to Community* (GA 257) where this process is described as the forming of new thinking and new willing.

[11] See the lecture of 19 December 1920 in *The Bridge Between Universal Spirituality and the Physical Constitution of Man* (GA 202).

[12] In the lecture mentioned above (note 9) Rudolf Steiner describes how the inner spirit and soul awakening through *The Philosophy of Freedom* is the only guarantee that man will be able to develop an inner sovereignty and independence in experiencing and representing Anthroposophy. He points out that, because of the failure to achieve this so far, the development of the Anthroposophical Society strays behind the development of the living anthroposophical stream.

his divergent soul forces and faculties in the concrete experience and action of life. The Ego of modern man comes to itself as a free and socially creative, loving self, only in this way. In any other way the consciousness soul shrivels and dies, and the lower soul parts degenerate or grow wild. The intellectual soul takes over thinking for itself, materializes it and deadens its living being, and the sentient soul is either overwhelmed by uncultivated feeling and will impulses or withers altogether. The warm life of the human heart, of feeling and fellow-feeling, the true foundation for the cultivation of modern spiritual science, remains undeveloped, and anthroposophical practice and social life become one-sided and antisocial.

This living grasp of spiritual science is not only necessary for developing free and creative human relationships, but also the most healthy and balanced foundation for the fully self-conscious entry of the consciousness soul into the spiritual worlds. For independent, thoroughly individualized supersensible experience and knowledge require the development of freedom and love no less than true social life on Earth requires them. For the true pupil of spiritual science, who experiences what man in our times can experience through deep participation in the inner and external events of the twentieth century, it can become an inner necessity to base his endeavours on this foundation of *The Philosophy of Freedom*. He knows that such a foundation enables the most conscious, clear and secure entry into the higher worlds.[13]

As a matter of factual experience, it can be discovered that when man begins to experience the supersensible life in pure thinking, even before the encounter with objective spirit reality, the experience varies considerably if he has prepared himself beforehand through the transformation of thinking into will and will into thinking, according to *The Philosophy of Freedom*. And the main difference consists in the fact that, through such a preparation,

---

[13] This problem is one of the essential themes of my multi-volume work *The Modern Christ Experience* (Amazon Kindle Direct Publishing 2024). See vol. 2 and vol. 3, entitled: *The Knowledge Drama of the Second Coming*.

the transition from daily consciousness to supersensible consciousness, as well as the maintaining of self-consciousness in
supersensible experience, is much closer in essence and practice to the nature of pure thinking, created in the preparation,
based on the actual transformation of thinking and will into one
another. In other words, here the way and goal of spiritual training are essentially the same from the very beginning, because
man lives already in the spiritual world in the true experience of
freedom and love.

The heightened state of consciousness, the soul and spirit
awakening out of the normal daily consciousness, which is the
true achievement of the schooling in *The Philosophy of Freedom*, is
then raised further upward. In this way a continuation of consciousness is realized that guarantees a great measure of freedom
and self-consciousness in supersensible experience, and thereby
also a greater capacity of memory in spirit of earthly identity
and, back in earthly consciousness, of the spiritual experiences.[14]

This spiritual-scientific way becomes especially necessary
when we consider those 'entirely new faculties' described by
Rudolf Steiner (see the next chapter), which have begun to make
their presence felt naturally in the soul of man in an ever-grow-
ing measure since the second third of the twentieth century. Here
we have to do with a direct streaming of spiritual events, processes and experiences into the naturally endowed human soul.
Such experiences, justified and beautiful as they are, must still
be thoroughly spiritualized if we want to make use of them in

---

[14] In *Occult Science* (GA 13) Rudolf Steiner characterized the unique position of *The Philosophy of Freedom* among the ways of spiritual training
as follows: 'These writings stand at an important point intermediate
between cognition of the sense world and that of the spiritual world
... Whoever permits these writings to act upon his entire soul nature,
stands already within the spiritual world ... He who feels himself in the
position to permit such an intermediate stage to act upon him travels a
safe path, and through it he is able to gain a feeling toward the higher
worlds that will bear for him the most beautiful fruit throughout all
future time.'

the service of spiritual-scientific research and daily living. Otherwise, precisely the best in them might be turned into its opposite and lead to a growing social and intellectual chaos, instead of into a deepened human social life and free thinking. And the best results in this sense are gained when these natural capacities and experiences are penetrated by the living and clear thought developed through *The Philosophy of Freedom*.

As Rudolf Steiner indicated, what we experience today as our pure thinking and individual freedom was experienced only after death in the former cultural epoch. It is an important secret of human evolution that what could only be experienced previously in the higher worlds, is increasingly streaming into the normal, wide-awake consciousness of humanity in the physical world.[15]

Now the Being and Advent of Christ Himself belongs to this secret, and is, from a certain point of view, at its heart.

Therefore, the Christ Event of the twentieth century, and of the future of the age of Michael and the consciousness soul age, falls together naturally with the growing of the human personality towards clear thinking, freedom, and love-permeated social life. The two events are essentially the same event, viewed from different perspectives. Both are symptoms of the growing spiritual maturity of the human soul, which comes gradually, through its natural development, to the point where its inmost spirit being on the one hand and conscious soul faculties on the other permeate one another increasingly in full self-consciousness.

When we bear in mind that the centre and source of the new supersensible soul faculties and experiences is the modern Christ Event, illuminated and guided by Michael, and further, that Rudolf Steiner repeatedly pointed to the inner, deep mutual relation between *The Philosophy of Freedom* and the Pauline Christ experience, then what we said above is seen in its true light. As we show in the second chapter of *The Modern*

---

[15] See the lecture of 30 January 1923, in *Awakening to Community* (GA 257).

Christ Experience, volume 1, Paul created, as the pioneer of the modern Christ experience, the 'Pauline method' of investigating the Christ Event,[16] which, carried in our time to its uttermost perfection for the age of the consciousness soul through Rudolf Steiner, remains the foundation for all future spiritualization of these faculties. The cognitive and moral freedom which man develops today naturally in the course of his daily life must come together more and more with the new supersensible soul forces and faculties. In this meeting spiritual science must rightly, and increasingly, intervene, because otherwise the new supersensible faculties are corrupted by both the intellectual-materialistic way of thinking and the wild growth of atavistic forms of clairvoyance. Also the best that is achieved through modern logical and free thinking can be destroyed by the new supersensible faculties running wild. This double aberration becomes a vicious circle, from which humanity will hardly escape without spiritual science:

> Even if people were able to have many super-sensible experiences, but disdained to apply healthy reason to them, these experiences would be of no use whatever to humanity in the future. On the contrary, they would do serious harm, for a super-sensible experience is of use only when it is translated into the language that human reason can understand. The real evil of our time is not that men have no super-sensible experiences; they could have plenty if they so wished. Such experiences are accessible, but healthy reason is not applied in order to reach them. What is lacking to-day is the application of this healthy human reason.[17]

Truly living and creative spiritual science is the only way to bring these two naturally given aspects of modern consciousness together into a fruitful, mutually upbuilding and strengthening interplay. This transformation of the naturally given sensible as well as supersensible consciousness was one of the most urgent

---

[16] See the lecture of 27 May 1914 (GA 152).
[17] See the lecture of 18 January 1920 (GA 196).

spiritual-scientific missions at the end of the last century and still is at the beginning of the our present one.

Modern spiritual science can fulfil this mission by becoming the truly living language of the present. It is possible to build the bridge from *The Philosophy of Freedom* to the Christ spirit, said Rudolf Steiner.[18] It is not our aim here to construct this bridge, described in detail in my books, *The Modern Christ Experience*, *Cognitive Yoga*, and *The Three Meetings*, but we are going to use it here in order to describe in some detail the Imagination of our century's greatest spiritual Event.

---

[18] See the lecture of 4 September 1917, in *The Karma of Materialism* (GA 176).

2

The New Soul Faculties: Rudolf Steiner's Indications

In the lectures delivered in 1910 in different branches of the Anthroposophical Society, mainly in Germany, Rudolf Steiner repeatedly drew attention to the coming time span of the thirties and forties.[19] In these years the Etheric Christ would begin to be visible to the new supersensible faculties that would begin to develop as a natural endowment, first among a few and then in an increasing number of people, in the next 2,500 years. We shall bring before us a characteristic indication from the lecture of the 25 January 1910 in Karlsruhe,[20] which offers a good summary of the main issues.

> The first signs of these new soul faculties will begin to appear relatively soon now in isolated souls. They will become clearer in the middle of the fourth decade of this century, sometime between 1930 and 1940. The years 1933, 1935 and 1937 will be especially significant. Faculties that now are quite unusual for human beings will then manifest themselves as natural abilities. At this time great changes will take place, and Biblical prophecies will be fulfilled. Everything will be transformed for the souls who are sojourning on Earth and also for those who are no longer within the physical body. Regardless of where they are, souls are encountering entirely new faculties. Everything is changing, but the most significant event of our time is a deep, decisive transformation in the soul faculties of man.

---

[19] In a lecture at Stuttgart on 6 March 1910 Rudolf Steiner mentions the years 1930-45, which include the 12 years that concern us. In Hanover, on 10 May 1910, he gives the time span 1930-50. Both lectures are in *The Reappearance of Christ in the Etheric* (GA 118).
[20] Ibid.

With these new soul faculties, whose development is clearly stated by Rudolf Steiner to be the most important of all the events he indicated, man will be able to perceive the Etheric Christ as a real supersensible Being in the etheric world. 'We must learn to understand,' says Rudolf Steiner, in the lecture at Stuttgart on 6 March 1910,[21] 'that in the future we are not to look on the physical plane for the most important events but outside it, just as we shall have to look for Christ on His return as etheric form in the spiritual world.' This means that the visibility of Christ is to be experienced in a special supersensible realm: His own world. In the lectures referred to here, Rudolf Steiner uses the Oriental designation 'Shamballa' to point to this special realm. For the initiates, he says, this land was also visible in the time of Kali Yuga: 'It is the same land to which initiates again and again repair in order to fetch from it the new streams and impulses for all that is to be given to humanity from century to century.'

Now this realm will become visible and available also to the naturally initiated:

> Humanity, through normal human faculties, will again grow into the land of Shamballa ... There is Shamballa; there was Shamballa; Shamballa will come to be again for humanity. Among the first visions that human beings will have, when Shamballa shows itself, will be Christ in His etheric form ... Christ will lead humanity to Shamballa.

Rudolf Steiner enthusiastically characterizes this land of Shamballa, into which more and more people will rise in the next 2,500 years, as 'light-woven, light-gleaming' and 'abounding in infinite fullness of life and filling our hearts with wisdom'. And 'The more visions human beings win for themselves, the greater Christ will appear to them, the mightier He will appear!'

---

[21] Ibid., and also the next three quotations.

In the lecture of 18 April 1910, in Palermo, Rudolf Steiner makes it clear that these naturally developing supersensible faculties will enable real initiation knowledge to develop.

Those human beings who experience the new 'Damascus Event' will have a direct knowledge of Christ: 'They will not require documentary evidence in order to recognize Christ, but they will have direct knowledge, as is today possessed only by the initiates. All the faculties that today can be acquired only by means of initiation will in the future be universal faculties of humanity. This condition of soul, this experiencing of soul, is called in esotericism the "second coming of Christ".'[22]

Furthermore, Rudolf Steiner repeatedly warns that this new development is fraught with great temptations, ordeals and crises. Therefore it will be a time of greatest decision. Until the beginning of the thirties, either humanity will have assimilated enough Anthroposophy for the Christ to be revealed through the new soul faculties, experienced and understood and thereby made into an upbuilding spiritual and social factor on the Earth, or humanity will not have done so. In the latter case, the way will be opened for the powers of evil that are preparing and awaiting such an omission. Briefly but clearly Rudolf Steiner indicated this tragic possibility at the end of his lecture in Berlin on 9 March 1910:[23]

> Thus humanity is called upon to decide whether or not it shall allow itself to be led into darkness even lower than that of Kali Yuga, ... [or] through an understanding developed by anthroposophy, it shall cultivate the new faculties by which it may find the way to the land of Shamballa ... that Christ will once more reveal. Such is the great decision to be made by men at the dividing of the ways. They must decide either to descend into something that, as a world-kamaloka lies deeper than Kali Yuga, or to work toward

---

[22] Ibid.

[23] In *The Christ Impulse and the Development of Ego Consciousness* (GA 116).

achieving what will enable them to enter the realm that is truly alluded to as Shamballa.

Rudolf Steiner offers a glimpse into the inner soul experiences and conditions out of which the new soul faculties are developing in two lectures at Dornach (30 and 31 October 1920).[24] Before the Second Coming, he says, 'all that remains of the old must be driven into the nullity ... The human being must find his full freedom out of the nothingness. And the new insight must give itself birth out of this nothingness. The human being must find his full freedom out of nullity.' And in the next lecture this situation of nullity is described further as a state of deep inner division of the human soul, out of which the new Christ experience will be made possible.

> This will be the solution of the most significant disharmony that has ever arisen in Earth-existence; the disharmony between the human being's feeling as an earthly being and his knowledge that he is a super-earthly being, a cosmic being. The fulfilment of this longing [*Drang*] will prepare man to recognize how, out of grey spiritual depths, the Christ-Being will reveal Himself to him and will speak to him spiritually, just as, at the time of the Mystery of Golgotha, He spoke to him physically. The Christ will not come in the spirit if human beings are not prepared for Him. But they can be prepared ... by sensing the discrepancy I described, by the schism weighing terribly heavily upon them from which they feel: 'I must regard myself as an Earth-being. Yet I am no Earth-being...'[25]

The last element that should be mentioned here, before we begin the actual description of the Imagination of the century's central spiritual Event, is indicated by Rudolf Steiner in a lecture on 25 October 1918 in Dornach. This indication touches the deepest

---

[24] Both lectures in *The New Spirituality and the Christ Experience of the Twentieth Century* (GA 200).

[25] Ibid., lecture of 31 October, 1920.

grounds of the new Revelation of the Etheric Christ in the twentieth century and is, therefore, of fundamental importance to our study here:

> Today when Christ is destined to appear again in the etheric body, when a kind of Mystery of Golgotha is to be experienced anew, evil will have a significance akin to that of birth and death for the fourth post-Atlantean epoch! In the fourth epoch the Christ impulse was born out of the forces of death for the salvation of mankind. We can say that we owe the new impulse that permeated mankind to the event on Golgotha. Thus by a strange paradox mankind is led to a renewed experience of the Mystery of Golgotha in the fifth epoch through the forces of evil. Through the experience of evil it will be possible for the Christ to appear again, just as He appeared in the fourth post-Atlantean epoch through the experience of death.[26]

During the last week of Rudolf Steiner's lecturing activity he directly alluded to the apocalyptic nature of the time beginning in 1933:

> The Beast will be released from its captivity in the Earth ... Before the Etheric Christ is recognized rightly by man, humanity must first come to terms with the confrontation with the Beast that comes out of the depths in 1933.[27]

---

[26] In *From Symptom to Reality in Modern History* (GA 185).
[27] In Lectures to Priests: *The Apocalypse, V* (GA 346), lecture of 20 September, 1924.

3

The Imagination of the Century's Event

Spiritually seen, the Second Coming of Christ in the etheric world, the centre of the century's Event, must be conceived as a totality, complete in itself, differentiated and accountable in terms of physical time measures only through the binding power of the historical drama of human evolution.

Essentially (that is, etherically) the Spiritual Event of the Twentieth Century should be thought of as an organic development and expression of the new revelation of the etheric Christ. Physically expressed, this means that the century's Event should be considered as beginning in the 12 years, 1933-1945, and extending over the whole century, 1933-1966-1999. However, because it answers the existential world question created in the 12 years, its centre can be located 'in the 12 years', as one speaks about the rhythmic system, based on the human heart and lungs, as the centre of the human constitution.

We shall have to bear this in mind, when we speak in this chapter of 'stages' or, better still, 'moments' of this Event, otherwise we shall misinterpret its essential nature and reduce rather than increase its healing, integrative power. Earthly time shows us in its succession only sequential, fragmented and isolated single aspects of that which always is a whole in the etheric, astral and spiritual worlds. That which is whole in itself can be grasped, however, only by Intuition, and not by the intellect, because Intuition is the 'higher thinking of the Spirit-Self';[28] the intellect is bound to the fragmented, isolated pieces of information that it laboriously collects, analyses and sums up in neat and ready-made conceptual constructions. Such a procedure, necessary

---

[28] Rudolf Steiner, *Theosophy* (GA 9), Chapter 2. In *The Philosophy of Freedom* (GA 4) intuitive thinking is regarded as a purely spiritual activity, by means of which man already lives as a thinker in the spiritual world, even before the first imaginative experiences.

and useful as it is in the physical, mechanical world, proves itself completely valueless and misleading in understanding the deeper levels of historical change and transformation.

Spiritual-scientific research in this field, therefore, must require from the investigator and reader alike a much greater readiness for productive, and intuitive, activity of thinking. Man must co-create with the working, formative spiritual forces active in the historical period of time into which he wishes to penetrate with his insight. The intellect rather passively waits for the events and later, after their happening, endeavours to collect them together and construct an abstract scheme of time references, using the common quantitative physical measurements of historical science, of economics, politics and sociology and so on, building always on that which is finished and past. In confronting the future, living but unknown, the intellect is powerless, because it can grasp only the results and not the motivating and forming forces that, in their living activity, shape history.[29]

But so it is also, of course, in regard to the true nature of the *past*. This past was once also an unknown future, springing out of the dark and, for the intellect, forever unfathomable and irrational complexities of human life. And as such it remains at present, an enduring riddle. But for an Intuition that can grasp these forces shaping history it is a living reality, accessible to the same spiritual-scientific research methods as the living future, because past and future alike are but two sides of a unified, timeless whole. The structure of this whole has its own unique causal connections with the earthly time dimensions and is related to

---

[29] As in other fields of scientific research, there exists a fruitful middle sphere between intellectual, brain-bound thinking and spiritual perception. Rudolf Steiner developed the method of 'Historical Symptomatology' (see GA 185) as a phenomenological-Goetheanistic method of approaching the study of history on the physical plane in the right way. Such a method prepares the ground for the results of imaginative perception, and combines with it in full harmony.

them in quite other ways than the linear causal logical schemes of the intellect.

Living, active Eternity had fertilized earthly time through the Mystery of Golgotha.[30] The Christ had prepared and then wholly penetrated and transformed human nature and human history in the 33 years of His earthly activity and sacrifice. He planted a seed of resurrection in the heart of time. This seed works rhythmically and germinates cyclically, revealing in time, for each human-historical deed, the true extent of its inner Christ nature.[31] Since the end of Kali Yuga it has begun to shape the course of history in the twentieth century. And the inner nature of the Event of the 12 years we are about to study is deeply connected with this Christ-filled life-rhythm of the Earth.

However, until the end of the century, the new Christ impulse could only reveal itself in the more external life of humanity, and not in the centre of the Michaelic movement. Since the 60s, it could be experienced in changes of consciousness and perception, related to the social, ecological and cultural life of humanity, moving from west to east.[32] Our purpose in this

---

[30] 'The Christ brought time back to humanity!' (see the lecture of 4 April 1924, in GA 236). According to Rudolf Steiner, it is the Christ force that lets everything mature in the womb of time. 'When within this transitory existence we grasp the Christ principle, these will mature for us; in the womb of the transitory, the intransitory, the eternal, the immortal. Out of the womb of time is born for us human beings that which is beyond time.' See *The East in the Light of the West* (lecture of 23 August 1909 in GA 113).

[31] 'For all things in historical evolution rise from the grave in changed form after 33 years, by the power that is connected with the most sacred, redemptive gift which humanity received through the Mystery of Golgotha.' See *Et Incarnatus Est* (lecture of 23 December 1917 in GA 180).

[32] This physical movement from west to east is an expression of an opposite spiritual stream that flows from east to west, calling the consciousness soul to an increasing spiritualization. See the lecture of the 10 June 1910 in *The Mission of Folk Souls* (GA 121) about the 'growing old' of humanity being bound up with the West and its youthful forces with the East. The true relation between West and East in our time is given in

book is to describe the Michaelic centre of this development, and let the new Christ impulse penetrate also into the core of spiritual science, otherwise, the fruitful social-peripheral forces must eventually decline. At the end of the twentieth century and the beginning of the twenty-first century, the anthroposophical 'mother field' itself must be resurrected, to fertilize and resurrect all aspects of human life.

From what grounds of human life spring those forces that can bring about a positive turn towards what is up-building and creative in the otherwise deeply distorted and exhausted human condition since the Second World War, intensified at the end of the century? We will have grounds to assume, after studying the occult significance of the Event of the 12 years, that this most tragic and destructive period of time conceals inwardly the greatest Mystery of our age as a whole, being spiritually the fountainhead of healing, courage and hope for the future of mankind's evolution.

The First Stage: Revelation

If the spiritual-scientific gaze is directed to the beginning of the second third of the century,[33] it is powerfully attracted to a

---

the second part of the Foundation Stone Meditation: 'Let there be fired from the East/What through the West is formed,/ Speaking:/ *In Christo morimur.*'

[33] A necessary preparation is a thorough identification with the earthly events of this period of human evolution. Man must totally immerse himself in the life and destiny of humanity as a whole, as well as of the single nations and single human beings in this span of time. For the years concerned here, it is especially significant to become inwardly one with the destiny of three peoples: Germans, Russians and Jews. The tragic karmic bonds that unite the three, when experienced in the light and warmth of the present Christ Revelation, reveals profound mysteries of the past, present and future destiny of the Christ impulse and the Ego development of humanity. (According to spiritual-scientific research, the Jews represent the past, the Germans the present, and the Russians the future of this impulse.)

certain point through which something wholly new begins to weave and sparkle in the etheric world. When the attention is focused on this point of time, a sudden, self-enhancing illumination is brought to consciousness. It breaks as if through a heavy foggy thicket; it lights up as a fiery glow. It bursts forth and expands in all time directions. In spreading it creates for itself a unique realm of appearance and existence. It unfolds an expanding movement that creates and enlivens space. Here something is shaping a realm for its revelation, intending it to be its homeland and kingdom. And this preparation gradually becomes itself the Revelation. In the centre of this ever inwardly expanding, radiating world, a figure takes shape. It is woven of the light rays of its own creation, and is aflame with the fiery tongues of its own unceasing, intensive self-burning. A universal, embryonic heart-centre is revealed. It forms itself in the midst of the otherwise heavily clouded and darkened planet Earth, teeming with infinite germinating seed vitality and activity. At the same time, it increasingly links its circulating pulse-beat with the Earth's enclosing cosmic periphery. The result is the creation of a network of luminous etheric blood veins and vessels. This network branches and differentiates itself like a living organism. It spreads its living roots, stems and leaves, knitting together centre and periphery of this universal becoming.

This insight reveals itself as having a strong inner affinity—the origin of which will be studied later—with man's imaginative activity and self-productive etheric organization. This means that the observer is not at all detached from the object of his observation, as in the physical world, but inwardly united with the Imagination described, and, moreover, that he knows himself to be an actual active participator in its birth. In the moment that man's attention is directed towards, and focused on, the central core of the Event, he is immediately there in living-time and knows himself to be part of that period of the twentieth century. His whole life organization becomes an instrument of pulsating light, receiving its rhythms from the living embryo at the core of the light-radiating Imagination. He knows that he is reverting thereby to his spiritual embryonic state of pre-earthly life. In the midst of the old, dying and darkened Earth, he knows himself as a part of the planetary womb of a new Sun becoming Earth.

The properly prepared spiritual scientist who undergoes such an experience does not lose himself in the greatness of this reality. He is able to control at will the speed and rhythm of his organization's expansion and contraction, and so establish the right balance of soul and life-forces needed for active imaginative observation. He is then aware of the help that is being granted him from the objective centre of his contemplation. He feels the unseen hands which turn his gaze to this direction or that, according to the requirements of his research, and enable him safely to grasp that which he is ripe to assimilate into his soul. And the more he grows into this new world of sprouting light the more he becomes conscious of the substantiality and reality of the Imagination described above. And even though he knows quite clearly that his insight is still rather abstract and external, he is also aware of the subtle ripening process that draws him inwardly ever nearer to the riddle of this new-born planetary kingdom.

When we penetrate this Imagination with the results of Rudolf Steiner's spiritual-scientific investigations concerning the cosmic, earthly and human Christ Mystery, past, present and future, we reach the following results. We realize that Rudolf Steiner's indications concerning the new Christ Revelation did come true, though ignored by man on the physical plane. The second third of that century did begin with the Revelation of a new supersensible realm in that world that is nearest to our physical world. The spiritual-scientific observation of this realm discovers that it is the result of almost two thousand years of hidden preparation. Since the Mystery of Golgotha the Sun power of Christ has been working in the heart of humanity and the Earth. In the heart of those human beings who were truly given to Him, He created the living substance needed for the building stones of the human temple of His Kingdom of the new Heaven and Earth. In the beginning of the second third of the twentieth century, it was made manifest what an advance was achieved in this work. Its Revelation clearly shows that, helped by the new Michael Impulse, the Christ could now gather its substance together and condense it to such an extent that a wholly Christ-permeated sphere of human activity and life could for the first time be made a planetary reality of the Earth. The Revelation shows the founding of Christ's own new human land and kingdom, the *true* Shamballa,[34] His new Heaven and new Earth, in which the life-giving source for all positive future earthly evolution is found.

In order to understand fully the nature of the change that revealed itself here, we must be aware of the fact that when Christ walked the Earth He did so among a mostly hostile and ignorant humanity. And though, of course, this is true also today—and in many respects in an even more drastic manner—a profound difference *does* exist. This difference is the result of the life and work of human beings who have united themselves with Him since the Mystery of Golgotha. It was possible for Him to establish a new, germinating Earthly-Sun Kingdom in the Earth itself. His Kingdom, which is not *of* this world, could strike deep roots *in* this world. And then those human souls who had participated in this work through the ages were again participators in the Revelation of the greatest spiritual Event in human evolution since the Mystery of Golgotha. They were to witness directly and actively the above described Revelation, at the time of its commencement, and were spiritually part of it in the life between death and rebirth.

---

[34] The luciferic occult streams of the East have made great efforts in the twentieth century to create a false, anti-Christian image of Shamballa in Western human consciousness. This began with the old Theosophical Society and continued in the teachings of Alice Bailey. Another branch of the same influence, concentrating its work more in Russia and eastern Europe, is described by Sergei O. Prokofieff in his book *The East in the Light of the West*, Part 1 (Temple Lodge Publishing, 1993).

We shall describe now the first stage of the Imagination of the century's central spiritual Event. We shall describe it as it was experienced by the small band of the disciples of Michael in the etheric world, who took an active part in its Revelation with light-filled spiritual consciousness and sight.[35]

In order to understand the part that those souls played, and still do today, in this supersensible Event, we shall have to point to some essential differences that exist between the ordinary relationship of the human soul to its spiritual surroundings and the special relationships and conditions that prevail in this case. In supersensible existence man not only develops the most intimate inner relationships with his world but also knows quite clearly that his self and the world around him are not at all as essentially different from one another as they are usually believed to be in the physical world. As the very ground of his self-experience in the spiritual worlds he knows that his own essence and substance is of the same essence and substance as the worlds in which he sojourns between death and rebirth. And if in the physical world the distance between subject and object, self and world, conditions all human physical consciousness and conduct, in supersensible reality the reverse is true. The self and its world with all its beings and processes are recognized to be rooted in the same primordial-divine origin. Man as a being of soul and spirit is submerged and carried in a soul-spiritual world, and his relation to this world is determined solely by the nature and quality of his inner affinities to this world.

Now in the new etheric world of the new Heaven and Earth, or Shamballa, we observe a special *enhancement* of

---

[35] This is the light of the new supersensible faculties that, as we saw in Chapter 2, were for the first time planted in human souls during these years. Therefore, when they are spiritualized on the Earth through anthroposophical spiritual science, they necessarily direct the spirit gaze to the 12 years. The soul faculties that were born at that time point, when matured, to their origin and illuminate it by means of the powers that created and shaped them.

these given conditions of any true spiritual existence. What is unusual here is the fact that the human soul feels this world as belonging to itself, and vice versa, in a still deeper sense. To the feeling of oneness with the external spiritual world is added here the clear perception that the life-element, which on the one hand constitutes one's own existence and on the other the substantiality of the external spiritual world, is in part of *human* origin. The enlivening warmth, light-and life-forces of this world, when inhaled and exhaled by the human soul as its own life-substance, are experienced as being of man's own making. They are a permanent result of the work of the whole Christ-permeated humanity on the Earth in former earthly lives.[36]

This is one exceptional aspect of the spiritual life of the human souls we are now considering. For the first time in human evolution the human race began to be a creative factor in cosmic and planetary evolution on which the gods themselves are counting in their future plans. This totally new step in human and earthly evolution is of the greatest significance for those who participate in the life of the Michael community established in the new Sun-sphere of the Earth.

Now let us remind ourselves of the imaginative picture of the Revelation described above, and let us consider it from the point of view of the human participators in this world Event. Our attention should be guided now not so much to the objective, external Imagination as such but rather to the occult nature of the creative process itself, which *brings about* this Revelation. And here we find the Michael pupils in their

---

[36] We mean here that which was described by Rudolf Steiner as the new etheric sphere. This has been created in the periphery of the Earth through the accumulation of the Christ-permeated, imperishable remains of human etheric bodies since the Mystery of Golgotha. (See *The Gospel of St John and its Relation to the Other Gospels*, lecture of 6 July 1909, in GA 112.)

supersensible Earthly-Sun work. We see them play their role in a threefold creative cycle:

1. assimilating into themselves;
2. penetrating the life-substance with their inner being;
3. reproducing, externalizing and moulding outwardly the world-creative, Christ-permeated human Imaginations into consistent and etherically permanent Sun formations.

They are actually helping to bring about a world birth, a world transformation of cosmic-planetary dimensions, in which a new embryonic Earthly-Sun centre is formed.

We see them, first, busy in gathering together the substance of two thousand years of Christ-permeated work on Earth. This is collected from the whole time (etheric) sphere of the Earth. Now, secondly, while recognizing in it their own preserved life-substance, they penetrate it with their strongest forces of self-conscious supersensible will and thought. Thirdly, as a result of this penetration process, this luminous mass is actively led towards the centre of the Earthly-Human Sun. There, at the centre, man observes how that which is humanly offered is accepted by the higher Sun Beings, and how they carry it still further to the inwardness of the becoming Earthly-Human Sun. There it becomes the nourishment of the world embryo described above, which is the heart-centre of Shamballa.

Cosmic thoughts and will impulses, anthroposophically grounded and steeled in the age of the consciousness soul on the Earth, bear in this way the most beautiful creative world fruit. They serve as the directing and formative forces with whose help alone the true spiritual achievement of humanity in the last two thousand years can proceed to its appointed goal. It is here that we learn to understand fully the absolutely indispensable world-forming power of every free anthroposophical thought and will impulse that was ever produced on the Earth, even in the most humble and simple life and achievement. Cognition is world-creating: creating is active world cognition in this world. The souls, at the summit of their world-shaping process, see and cognize while creating how the new world's embryo is actually transformed through this work.

The nature of this transformation is revealed the more the work proceeds. It grows and matures and increases its light and life rhythms. But this means also that man shapes increasingly the sheaths of the Christ Being Himself. Human creation and His life and appearance merge as never before in human evolution.[37]

The deepest spirit joy and strongest, invincible courage is planted in the human soul when it contemplates with holy awe these mysteries. For it is really true to say that, for the first time since Christ's sacrifice for the Earth and humanity, He found a small yet tested and dedicated group of human souls who work consciously to bring about the fulfilment of His will and sacrifice on the Earth and in Heaven. To experience in active spirit existence that the further development of His objective world Being is dependent on human efforts, and to see, in creating, how He rejoices in receiving that which enables Him to advance His work, is the most sublime human aspect of the Revelation we have described so far.

In order to appreciate fully the novelty of the century's Event, however, we must penetrate still deeper into its occult nature. This penetration is brought about when we re-awaken in us the inner soul and spirit experiences of those who participated in the Revelation. These experiences slumber in each anthroposophical soul in its earthly life today. They can be awakened and raised to consciousness through the training and research methods of spiritual science. Let us, then, delve deeper into these world-transforming events.

---

[37] This supersensible human work at Shamballa is another aspect of what was described by Rudolf Steiner as the forming of Christ's new sheaths through human forces. (See lecture of 8 May 1912 (GA 143) and *Earthly and Cosmic Man* (GA 133), lecture of 14 May 1912).

Up to now, the description of the first stage of the century's Event was only partial, and contained only one side of its real nature. The other, to begin with unseen and hidden side, eludes our attention. It shies away from the searching spirit gaze. Man feels also a strong inner resistance that arises from the depths of the soul, as if wishing instinctively to protect itself from a sight that, in ordinary daily consciousness, it would be unable to endure. Only the repeated identification with the light-filled side of the Revelation described above, with the infinite moral strengthening that it offers, enables man to uncover that which lies deeply covered in his unconscious soul depths.

A veil is torn away from man's eyes, and the etheric light ground of the new world becomes unexpectedly turbulent and insecure. Then it disintegrates and falls away altogether. But man is one with this world. Therefore, its falling away opens a bottomless, dark abyss under his spirit feet. Suddenly, man hovers dangerously over what is the total opposite of everything to which he adheres above with all the fibres of his higher being. At the place where there was the living and ensouled Earth, there now appears a vast monstrosity. It seems to strive to the heights in order to pull those heights down and devour them. When we bear in mind that in supersensible reality the human soul reacts in quite other ways than in the physical world to the most shocking experiences, nevertheless we must characterize this moment as the greatest soul-and-spirit shock that man can have in our age.

The situation described here can be adequately grasped only if we form a spiritual-scientific picture of the essential being of 'Michaelic Man', which, taken as the Higher Self of the small Michael community, lives also in each of its single members as a special, individual higher self. This being is 'the human being Anthroposophia', born in the Christmas Foundation Conference in 1923, and taken with Rudolf Steiner to the etheric world in 1925. Such a Self is that being to which we referred above when we sought to indicate the measure of the identification and active participation of those human souls in the century's Event. It is a Christ-like being, united with the destiny of humanity and the Earth as a whole. This being now experiences the Revelation as the deepest division of its *own* inmost being. This is an unprecedented experience in human evolution. Never before has it been possible for fully individualized human beings to experience such a cosmic, earthly and all-human split as a *self*-experience. And this is the truly unforgettable Michael-Christ experience at the first stage of our century's central spiritual Event.

The loyally remaining Michael pupils felt the most tragic soul bewilderment and helplessness in the face of this split because of its *simultaneous* occurrence with the highest Revelation of spirit communion and oneness. This tremendous inner paradox and self-contradiction was caused by a fissuring of the whole new Earthly-Human Sun being. And out of humanity's helplessness in the face of the evil surfacing from the abyss, threatening total self-destruction, there emerged a mighty soul-and-spirit mood. But before we describe the nature of this experience we shall first prepare the ground for its understanding by means of the following spiritual-scientific consideration.

In the ordinary course of life after death, the human soul passes through Kamaloka in the Moon-sphere and leaves behind it after purification its 'lower self' containing all the forces of hindrance and destruction that would have made any further ascent into the spirit world impossible. Then man passes through the higher regions of the soul world and enters the spirit world through the gate of the Sun as a purely spiritual being, or 'higher self'. And only after a long preparation, which consists mainly in the forming of the next earthly life in accordance with the laws of karma, attaining its culmination in what Rudolf Steiner called 'the cosmic midnight hour of existence', does man return to the Earth. He descends to birth through the gate of the Moon and integrates his lower self— which had been kept there for him through the sacrificial grace of the higher Moon beings— into his whole being according to the wisdom-filled guidance of his karma.[38]

Now all this takes place, for the human soul in our age, only by virtue of the care and protection of the hierarchical beings who watch over human evolution. The separation of the lower self from the higher, and the much later unification of the two, occurs through strict, wholly transcendent laws to which the soul is readily obedient. This background may enable us to look into the hidden occult process that took place at what must be called the *planetary midday hour* of the Michael School in the etheric world of the Earthly-Human Sun in the second third of the twentieth century. This unsual designation must be used, because it took place precisely at the moment in which the Revelation of the new Sun of the etheric Christ appeared in all its planetary midday glory.

The occult significance of this planetary Michaelic midday hour is that it coincided with the division Event in the destiny of humanity as a whole; that is, with the separation of humanity and the Earth into two wholly separated higher and lower selves. This, as we indicated above, was experienced in the most spiritually shattering manner by the Michael pupils. But the shattering was all the greater because they realized that what was possible in their own unique existence and destiny was *not* taking place in the existence and destiny of humanity as a whole. While they consciously underwent their own spiritual metamorphosis and rebirth, and participated in the exceptionally condensed separation and reunion of their higher and lower selves, they became all the more aware of the fact that humanity as a whole has failed to master the same initiatory process through conscious anthroposophical activity on the Earth in the first third of the century. And this deeply fissured situation of humanity now became their own divided Earth-ly-Human Sun existence and destiny precisely *at the highest*

---

[38] See, for example, the lecture of 16 May 1924 in *Karmic Relationships* Vol. II. (GA 236)

moment of their planetary midday hour of existence. They saw
and experienced the *division* of humanity in, through, and as,
their unique Michaelic destiny. Their own newly gained spiritual wholeness in the living and radiant Earthly-Human Sun-
sphere of Christ's new etheric revelation was transformed 'at
the very moment' into its complete opposite: into the darkest
and deepest division experience and situation of humanity.
Here personal and collective human destiny became in reality
two aspects of one and the same event.

In this sense the comprehension of the century's Event is
essentially deepened. We realize that for the small Michael
community sojourning in the nascent etheric sphere of the new-
ly-born Earthly-Sun, the karma of the world and mankind and
personal karma became one. The occult role of this group of souls
in future world evolution consists in the struggle to achieve this
oneness. The most potent seed for the future possibility of fulfill-
ing this goal was now created.

Now we are in a position to come back to the decisive self-
split and self-contradiction indicated above. As pointed out
above, the eventual reunion of man's returning higher self
with the lower self, left behind in the Moon-sphere, is safe-
guarded and regulated according to the infinite loving wisdom of world divine being and becoming, which carries the
individual soul and brings it securely to its destined incarnation. What happens unconsciously in the life of the human
soul, becomes a conscious soul experience for the Initiate. But
humanity *as a whole* is now the World Initiate; unconsciously
it has been crossing the threshold of the spiritual world since
the middle of the *last* century. But it ought to have been, before
the middle of the *twentieth century*, in the position to undergo
consciously its division and reunion as a healthy, initiatory
process. This means to confront its Lower Guardian, that
appears in the imagination of the first apocalyptic Beast, and
recognize him for what he is. However, this is precisely what
did not happen. But according to the strict rules of initiation,

an unlawful—because unconscious—crossing of the threshold must lead to self-destruction.[39]

Humanity stood now at the most crucial moment of its present initiation. From the spiritual world, its destructive disorientation at the moment of its initiation breakthrough was experienced in fully conscious spirit sight. There, the *true* state of affairs was seen and understood. The small band of souls, that remained true to Michael, whose unique destiny we have been following, stood before the gravest situation ever experienced by human beings in the course of human evolution. They realized that in

---

[39] Since the middle of the last century, humanity has passed beyond the threshold of the spiritual world while refusing to confront consciously its Lower Guardian. But, as Rudolf Steiner warned, humanity 'for its own good, must look back and take note of him [the Guardian]. For to continue not heeding him, to live on into the following centuries without heeding him, would lead mankind to complete disaster.' (Lecture of 12 January 1924 in *Rosicrucianism and Modern Initiation*, GA 233a.)

Such a disaster befell humanity during the 12 years. In order to fully understand what actually took place, we must remember that in the future vision of Earth evolution described by Rudolf Steiner in *Occult Science, An Outline* in the year 1909, the problem of evil self-consciously perpetrated was still an *open possibility*. While an evil sub-human race will appear in the future as an outcome of the pre-individualized human evolution of the past, it might be possible, so he writes, that no human egos will have created such an evil *personal karma* that they will be obliged to incarnate in such bodies. It might be necessary for beings from other evolutionary streams to incarnate in the evil race, because human beings would be too good for it. Now the world event described above, and its shattering Michaelic experience, is rooted in the fact that, since the events of the 12 years, the possibility that was still open at the beginning of the twentieth century is no longer open. A leading group of human beings did individualize evil in the age of the consciousness soul evolution, and this means that they have begun consciously to burden their karma with the greatest possible human evil. The clear perception of this fact lies at the centre of the Michaelic experience of the Imagination of the century's Event.

the wisdom-filled, loving cosmic guidance of humanity there is no existing, naturally given power that will intervene from outside in order to correct for humanity that which was disastrously corrupted through human ignorance, pride and cruelty. For them the sublime Revelation showed itself to be the greatest wholeness on the one hand yet on the other a tormenting split of self, mankind and the world.

If we contemplate this Imagination—and many years of intensive meditative practice were required before this could have been accomplished—we can grasp the first stage of last century's spiritual Event, when we investigate its occult significance in the light of spiritual science. We realize that the new *Revelation of the Etheric Christ is deeply divided.*

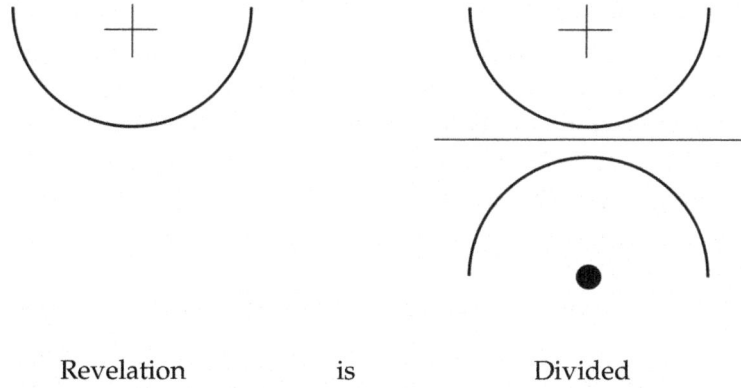

Revelation   is   Divided

The Second Stage: The Great Sacrifice

This is, then, the situation of humanity actually *beyond* the threshold, viewed from the nearest spiritual world to the Earth. It is a tragic view, comparable only with the picture of a false, misguided initiation, which results, among other things, as Rudolf Steiner described it in his book *Occult Science*, in the 'occult captivity' by the Lower Guardian of the Threshold.[40] In this captivity the disciple not only falls prey to his illusions but entirely

---

[40] Rudolf Steiner, *Occult Science, An Outline*, Chapter 5 (GA 13).

reverses the truth of the Lower and Higher Guardians. He experiences the loving, healing, bestowing approach of the Higher Guardian—that is, the Christ Himself—as if He is the Lower Guardian, in boundless dread. And, consequently, humanity also worshipped the Lower Guardian as the saviour: the Higher Self. Man believes that the Christ is his greatest enemy and fights Him with all his might, which must lead dangerously close to complete suicidal self-destruction. From this aspect we see that, if the situation of humanity in the 12 years, 1933-45, had remained just what it came to be through the divided and reversed situation of the Revelation, it must necessarily have ended in total world disaster.

All this was, as described, seen and understood by those who could follow these events consciously from beyond the threshold. They stood now, as was said above, before the gravest situation ever experienced by individualized and free human beings during the whole course of human evolution.[41] Let us try to grasp the occult significance of this situation, and what was developed out of it, in the light of spiritual science. It is this situation and the dramatic events that resulted from it which leads to the central core of the century's Event as a whole, which must be named the 'Great Sacrifice'.

The small Michael community confronted this situation, the riddle of our time, on two levels: first, as one single spirit-individuality, the human being Anthroposophia, in the fullest consciousness and freedom; and second, in each of its single members, though, of course, in different degrees of conscious individual participation. Coinciding with the Revelation of

---

[41] This situation of humanity can also be described in the following words: 'The judgment begins from our twentieth century on, that is, the ordering of karma.' (Lecture entitled 'Faith, Love, Hope', 2 December 1911, GA 130.) Also: 'This indeed is the time of great decisions, the great crisis to which the sacred books of all time have referred, for in reality our own age is meant.' (Lecture of 3 August 1924 in *Karmic Relationships* Vol. III, GA 237.)

Christ's new Kingdom, His new Heaven and Earth on the one hand, there emerged, out of the dark earthly abyss below, the being who must be seen as Christ's absolute opposite, His most evil and hate filled enemy. This being was revealed in his own new sub-earthly kingdom. And these two kingdoms stood over against each other, the one ruling above but ignored and attacked from below, the other gaining increasing control over the earthly affairs of blinded humanity.

Seen imaginatively from above, and experienced as the schism of man's all-human self, humanity and the Earth take on the form of a deeply wounded, bleeding, poisoned and mutilated being. It suffers with no hope of recovering. It strives to extinguish itself and so escape its spiritual responsibility. It is unable either to heal itself or to put an end to its tormented existence. Anthroposophia, 'Michaelic Man', now experiences, as described above, Her unity with the Earth and all its kingdoms and creatures and with mankind as a whole. She is identified wholly with the Christ Being who revealed Himself in His new Heaven and Earth as humanity's higher Self. Now, in the midst of this tremendous self-conflict, experiencing morally the greatest helplessness of wounded, divided humanity and planet Earth, the human being Anthroposophia must find a surplus of moral-spiritual power in order to transform Her experience into a healing power, that She can offer as redeeming *answer* to humanity's existential *question*.

But how can we form an adequate concept of the nature of this universal existential human 'question'? To begin with, on Earth, we can try to grasp it in our *feelings* through its deeply moving moral quality. But how is it actually, practically formed in supersensible life and activity in the Earthly-Human Sun-sphere? Above we described the nature of the work being done by the Michael pupils in Christ's new world. We saw them gathering, condensing, reproducing and shaping the humanly-created Christ-permeated life-substance that streams from Earth to Heaven. They offered it to the Beings of the higher hierarchies, who transformed and moulded it further. And then, in a sacred human-angelic ritual, it was offered up on the altar in the Earthly-Sun temple.

However, *this* sacred ritual comes at this moment to a sudden end; it is abruptly halted by the deepening division of humanity and Earth. And this arrested cultus, marks the beginning of the second stage of the century's Event. A long moment of cosmic silence follows. It seems that everything is paralysed and frozen in the new land of everlasting, burgeoning Earthly-Sun life. At that moment, for the first time in two thousand years, humanity has entirely forgotten the Christ impulse; in human consciousness and life on Earth, *there was nothing left of the Earth's upward-flowing Christ-permeated life-substance and nourishment.* The former life source of the creative building process of the new Earthly-Human Sun was exhausted. In its stead the evil form of humanity surfaced out of the abyss below. This abyss opened itself inside the obsessed and seduced being of self-conscious humanity and Earth.

This was the decisive time of trial and decision. The purely human aspect of the spiritual Being of Anthroposophia was tested. It had to find now truly free moral power in order to take upon itself the karma of humanity. It turned its sacrificial will to the wounded humanity on Earth. Michaelic Man, active in the spirit hearts of its human members, responded to the upstreaming cry of humanity. They poured their soul and life-forces downward and received into their hearts the millions of murdered, tortured and slaughtered souls that increasingly made their way upward from the great tribulation below. These souls were passing through the gates of death in a state of great inner disturbance. They carried in their souls a burning, desperate *question* about the nature and future of man and human life and existence in this darkest period of human evolution. The question that humanity refused to ask freely in the age of the consciousness soul, namely, the question about the nature and being of man himself, Anthropos, *the question about Anthropos-Sophia,* was finally asked—but asked through the deepest experience of evil.

In the midst of this unprecedented world situation stood the small band of souls in between their own personal death and rebirth. They were destined to experience the shattering gap holding sway between the extreme poles of the highest life and evil death of humanity. And they could not see any given, pre-ordained salvation. Now their own, independent moral strength had to prove its spirit maturity.

They opened their hearts to the upstreaming pain, anguish and despair of so many millions of fellow human beings. They actively imbued their higher Michaelic being with the etherized blood of all races and nations on the bleeding Earth. This act ignited this etherized, universally-blended human blood with the fire of their compassion and love for mankind. *A mighty moral flame shaped itself in the etheric world.* They articulated it into the human World-Answer-Word while standing face to face with the greatest evil ever to appear on the stage of human evolution.[42]

They thus linked the oldest moral bond of humanity, now annihilated in the burning evil below, with the highest future goal of humanity residing in the being and consciousness of Christ. They raised their divided all-human self as an offering on that altar whose fire alone can withstand the storms of wildest evil. They *became* the answer to the question of world and human evolution, and wrote it with fiery letters in the astral light sphere of the Earthly-Human Sun. This offer of all-embracing human love will abide with humanity and the Earth until the last of its fallen creatures is redeemed.

---

[42] The central situation of the Michael community in the 12 years can therefore rightly be understood as its Grail ordeal and initiation. That which was celebrated prophetically, in mighty *pictures,* in the Michaelic cultus at the end of the eighteenth and the beginning of the nineteenth centuries, became here spirit reality. The power gained through the founding of Anthroposophy in the physical world was now used to endure this trial and secure the future of human evolution.

This work can be described from still another aspect. Through the evil enacted on the Earth, a situation was created in which a real Hell ('World Kamaloka' as Rudolf Steiner called it) came into being. For the first time in human evolution, some human beings entirely lost their primordial humanness. An earthly kingdom was established in which the divine image of man was systematically reversed and replaced by its opposite. The truth that animated all religions and cultures, expressed most clearly in the Book of Genesis in the Bible and in the first chapter of the Gospel of St John, namely, that humanity as a whole was created in the image of God through the Logos—the Christ—as *one* whole being, was now suppressed and practically reversed. For the first time, millions of human beings lived and died in such a way that they experienced man as a totally different creature, shaped not in the image of God through Christ but in the image of the Lower Self of humanity. As a result, *the ancient bond of the human race*, the inherited life-blood of creation, that was mainly flowing through the blood stream of the ancient Jewish people, *was annihilated*. It's primordial heart-centre, the carrier of its inherited, God given 'I', was attacked and physically and etherically destroyed.[43] As a

---

[43] Here we touch upon mysteries of the 12 years that cannot at the present time be openly communicated, because the necessary good will, required for true moral self-knowledge, is still lacking in humanity. Only when the *reality* of the Imagination of our century's Event is consciously understood, and, at least in the life of a small group of human beings, is also practically realized on the Earth, will it be possible to begin to speak more directly about it. The following indication must therefore suffice. We have to be reminded at this point that, according to spiritual science, it was the evolutionary role of the ancient Hebrew people to prepare and carry the inherited bloodstream through which the physical, bodily foundation of the incarnating, cosmic Higher Self of humanity, the Christ, was created. (See, for example, GA 117 and GA 123.) It was this past hereditary bloodstream that now came under the most concentrated conscious attack of evil. (At the same time, achieving

result, humanity ceased to be one united being and became deeply divided, as was shown above.

Now, at the very moment when this truth was perceived above, a new embryonic heart-organ for the *future* unity of divided humanity had to be created. It was now the task of the small band of souls, that remained loyal to the Michael School, by making the destiny of divided humanity into its own destiny, to shape this future embryonic heart-centre of humanity out of its own life-substance. An etheric heart-organ of the future Michael-Christ race of humanity was now created, in place of the ancient, dying heart-organ, prefiguring for all ages to come the higher unity of the human race, through which evil shall gradually be transformed into the highest good. And this new embryonic heart, created through the etheric life-blood of the human being Anthroposophia, stretching from above downward, bridged the abyss between the two separated parts of humanity and the Earth. What humanity failed to achieve through conscious anthroposophical work on the Earth in the first third of the twentieth century was now prefigured spiritually in the etheric world *after* the great apocalyptic division of humanity and the Earth. And only when this new bridging heart-organ was established could the Christ Himself join the work of redemption with His renewed sacrifice.

Then the Michael pupils could see how, out of the innermost core of the temple of the Earthly-Human Sun, a Being comes

---

during the 12 years some of its most destructive forms, the second arm of the same evil—Bolshevism—attacked the future bearers of the Christ impulse and Ego development of humanity, while the *present* foundation of the Christ impulse and Ego development of humanity, namely Germany itself, was attacked directly at its source through its own spiritual self-denial and capitulation. On the occult nature of National Socialism, see the three pioneer lectures of J. Tautz, *1933-Rückschau und Ausblick*, Johanni, 1966. About the occult nature of Bolshevism, see the detailed research of S.O. Prokofieff in his book *The Spiritual Origins of Eastern Europe and the Future Mysteries of the Holy Grail* (Temple Lodge Publishing, 1993), especially the second and third parts.

forth, no longer only an embryo of future evolution. Nurtured and matured through human acts of sacrifice, He made His way from the heights of His etheric Revelation downward, crossing the Michael bridge from Heaven to Hell. As His pathway He used the etherized bloodstreams that ascended, spiritualized in the new heart-centre of humanity, from the evil abyss below. They could follow Him with their spirit gaze. He descended ever deeper, until He merged Himself completely with the evil being of humanity in the abyss, blending His downpouring life, soul and spirit forces with that being. In their upward striving sacrifice, carrying to Him the etherized pain of the nations of the world, they beheld Him sinking ever deeper into the core of burning human evil, uniting Himself with it and dying livingly into the densest point of its being. They witnessed thus the culmination of the second Mystery of Golgotha at the moment of its happening.[44]

As a result of the development of the Michael stream at the end of the century, man can consciously make the spiritual Event of the twentieth century into a part of his life and soul. The true question of this century—which is about the whole future of human evolution—can be made our own if we bear it consciously. It was experienced as follows: if that which happened in the first stage of the Event during the 12 years on the Earth and in Heaven remains as it is, humanity and the Earth will be ever more divided into two halves. These halves will speed away from one another in opposite cosmic direc-

---

[44] This is the continuation and fulfilment of Christ's second Mystery of Golgotha, His 'Manichaean' sacrifice that began at the end of the nineteenth century. (See lecture of 2 May 1913 in *Occult Science and Occult Development*, GA 152). Then He assimilated into Himself the materialistic thoughts of the human beings who passed through the gate of death. Out of this sacrifice in the twentieth century, the 'Christ-consciousness' of man in our time is created. Now He assimilated also man's primordial evil being. Out of this sacrifice a still higher force will develop in human beings in the future: the moral courage and sacrifical love that will transform evil into the highest good.

tions, tearing humanity's soul-and-spirit unity apart, with no hope of eventual reunion. The Michaelic dilemma outlined above was that no solution could be offered from the farthest reaches of the cosmos to this wholly new human situation. Completely new forces of the human soul and spirit had to be *created*.

Now, when they identified themselves with the situation of earthly humanity, the souls who remained true to Michael prefigured, in their planetary Earthly-Sun life, the great Sacrifice of Christ. They walked again in His steps as they did in former earthly lives, only now the order of following was reversed. They went *before* Him, showing *Him* the way, acting out of free and self-conscious *human* decision, and He followed in their steps only after they fully united themselves with the divided karma of Earth and humanity. Only then could He offer His sacrifice as the answer to the new, future question of human existence: the question concerning the mission and fate of evil.

It is here that we can clearly grasp the change that has taken place in human evolution in the last two thousand years. While the Mystery of Golgotha was an act of pure divine grace bestowed on humanity from above, to which *uninitiated* humanity had nothing to add, in the culmination of the second Mystery of Golgotha it had—as part of the destiny of the Michael stream—a decisive role to play.[45] And this will be ever more the case in all future battles and crises of Earth evolution.

Since the end of the twentieth century, what was achieved in

---

[45] Rudolf Steiner repeatedly pointed out that the Mystery of Golgotha was an act of divine grace that had to counter-balance the primeval luciferic temptation and fall of pre-individual humanity. The luciferic intervention and its results did not create, therefore, a karmic debt on the part of man himself, because it originated out of much larger cosmic necessities reaching far beyond the time of man's individuation and self-conscious moral responsibility. It was this debt that was taken on by Christ through His free deed of love. (See, for example, the lecture entitled 'The Concepts of Original Sin and Grace', of 3 May 1911, GA 127.)

the supersensible life and existence in the etheric world, must find its expression in the fully conscious activity of the Michaelic movement on Earth. What was made real in spirit by the true pupils of Michael must now be humbly translated into a down-to-earth readiness to manifest these forces in day-to-day physical and social life, in order to make Christ's Sacrifice increasingly true on the physical Earth. This had first to be raised to full anthroposophical consciousness at the end of *last* century, in order to be practised in *this* century by the new Michael movement and School on the Earth, out of the free and earthly consciousness of incarnated men and women.

This is, then, the occult core of the Imagination of our century's Event: *the Michaelic answer to the universal human question becomes the great Sacrifice.* That is, the culmination of the second Mystery of Golgotha occurs through modern evil. (See diagrams on page 51.)

The Third Stage: Birth of the Earthly-Human Sun

If what we said about the nature of the century's Event in relation to time is borne in mind, we may proceed to describe 'the third stage' without misguidedly assuming that these stages are successive events in earthly time that follow one another in linear sequence. That we do, after all, describe them as such—that is, as separate, causally-linked stages—is only because we shall later try briefly (see Chapter 5) to connect them with the earthly time span of the 12 years. This will be done in order to find the right way to understand the true relation between these years and the events that took place in the physical world at the 'same' time. This means, therefore, that our basic threefold division of the century's Event into Revelation, Sacrifice and Earthly-Human Sun-Birth is done in view of the earthly events of the 12 years. Bearing this carefully in mind, we may advance to the following observations.

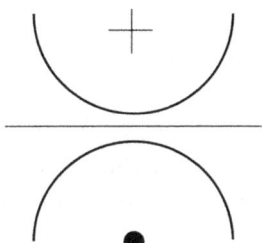 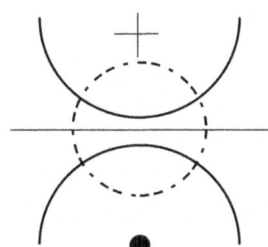

Divided Revelation   Heart-centre: Michael Bridge

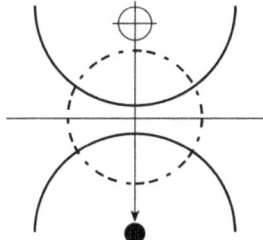

The Great Sacrifice

The third stage completes the whole Event and makes it into a self-contained living and breathing totality. For imaginative observation the Earth appears now as a living, ensouled and spiritual planetary being, as an Earthly-Human Sun, an astral and etheric cosmic organism in its own right. It is actually only when we repeatedly contrast this end result (as 'third stage') with the 'first stage', which culminated in the great splitting of humanity and the Earth, that we find our way to penetrate into the mysteries of its 'second stage' described above, which are the most hidden from sight.

Christ's Manichaean demonstration of infinite love and sacrifice is the future archetype of all transformation and redemption of evil in our universe. That which He suffered and overcame through His becoming one with humanity's evil being belongs to the things that cannot yet be grasped by earthly, human cognition. Humanity must evolve morally much further before even a preliminary attempt to penetrate this Mystery will be possible. But when we observe the visible *etheric results* of Christ's unfathomable Sacrifice, we are comforted by the realization that from now on His eternal being germinates and grows for humanity in the core of all evil.

The result of what we lost sight of in the sub-earthly depths below comes back to us from the entire circumference. It appears in its imaginative reflection as light-radiating spirit holiness from the expanding circumference of the Earthly-Human Sun. That is, at the unseen moment of the merging of Christ with the primordial evil being of humanity, *the upper kingdom of the Earthly-Human Sun, until now separated from its lower, demonized self, turned inside out and around and embraced its lost half of self.* It thus became one cosmic body, carrying in its centre that which was formerly outside itself. This part would have become ever more separated from it if the human-Michaelic sacrificial answer and Christ's sacrificial deed had not been consummated. This healing deed, of the deeply fissured self, will be borne consciously from the twentieth century onward as the germinal healing of the inwardly burning wound of humanity's evolution. The turning of Shamballa inside out and around had surrounded the whole Earth with a glorious but inwardly humble holy illumination. This light is the youthful, new life radiation of the Earthly-Human Sun.

The imaginative gaze observes how, for the first time in the evolution of the Earth, since its separation from the Old Sun, but now as an independent being, it becomes an outwardly radiating, cosmic Earthly-Human Sun being. But what does it actually mean to become a cosmic Sun being?

Being 'Sun' means, whether macrocosmically or microcosmically, two related things. First, a Sun being is one who can guide and carry consciously, independently, his 'lower self' through the love and wisdom of his 'higher self'. He takes full responsibility for the regulation of his own karma, and begins to transform its evil into a higher good. This means, secondly, that such a being is transformed from a receiving into a giving one, from a being dependent on the life and light of others to a source of life and light *for* other beings and worlds. He becomes a life-giving, light-radiating 'Sun'. He begins to offer surplus of his creative power to other, less evolved beings, as once he himself was cared for by higher Sun beings.

The Earth could be born as a new Sun in the middle third of the century because its Higher Self, the Christ, was so deeply accepted by a representative group of free human beings. These are the true pupils of Michael in the age of the consciousness soul, as we showed above. They could take upon themselves the karma of humanity out of free moral Intuition, Inspiration and Imagination. Christ's Sacrifice was then the macrocosmic counterpart of their microcosmic-planetary Sun act of moral freedom in face of the evil being of humanity. It was the first *fully conscious* co-operation between a free representative group of humanity, representing its upward aspiring earthly self, which ascends to the etheric heights of the Earthly-Human Sun, and its all-embracing, descending Higher Self, the Christ. He acted upon their sacrificial answer to the burning question of wounded humanity, with His mighty descent into humanity's seduced lowest being. *And this co-operation and mutual penetration between the higher and lower selves of humanity and Earth is the occult cause and significance of the Sun-Birth of the Earthly-Human Sun in the etheric universe.*[46]

---

[46] The supersensible Michaelic experience of the renewing of the Mystery of Golgotha through evil, described here, can be compared now with the supersensible Michaelic experience of the Mystery of Golgotha itself. The last was described by Rudolf Steiner as follows: 'We were united with Michael in the realm of the Sun. Christ, who hitherto had sent His impulses towards the Earth from the Sun, departed from the Sun in order to unite Himself with earthly evolution. Try to picture to yourselves this stupendous cosmic event that took place in realms

It consummated the greatest Event of the apocalypse of the present Michael age at the dawn of the new cosmic age of light and the Second Coming. Earth and humanity were born again as an evolving fixed star: a new Sun-Star was born in the universe. The Earth and humanity as a whole passed through its first stage of conscious initiation and became a Christ-permeated, holy planet. The sacred work of transforming evil into the highest good had begun. This is the third stage which completes the century's Event: the Earth becomes a new Sun-Star through humanity's conscious and free collaboration with its Higher Self, the Christ.

---

beyond the Earth: it lies within the mighty vista open to those human souls who at that time were gathered around as servants of the Angeloi, after His rulership on Earth had ended. In the realm of the Sun they witnessed the departure of the Christ from the Sun. "He is departing!" . . . such was their great and overwhelming experience when He left in order to unite His destiny with the destiny of earthly humanity.' (See *Karmic Relationships* Vol. VI, lecture of 19 July 1924, GA 240.) Also: 'When the cross was raised on Golgotha and the blood flowed from the wounds of Christ Jesus, a new cosmic centre was created. We were there when that occurred: we were present as human beings, whether in a physical body or outside this physical life between death and rebirth.' (See *The Gospel of St John and its Relation to the Other Gospels*, lecture of 6 July 1909, GA 112.) To this description of the first Mystery of Golgotha we can now add the following testimony concerning the second. We were indeed again present there, but not now above in the old Sun realm, but here, on the etheric Earth itself, becoming the Earthly-Human Sun, when the cosmic centre as an embryonic star-seed was completed. We did not watch Christ's descent from the Sun to the Earth, while remaining behind in the Sun-sphere. We observed His descent into the depths of human evil, making His way across the abyss of humanity that opened itself *inside* our own Michael-Christ, all-human self. Now we ourselves, who have matured through the great spirit battles of the last two thousand years in the service of the Michael-Christ impulse, constructed the Michaelic heart-bridge of resurrected humanity, through which the Christ could fulfil His second, post-Golgolthean sacrifice. From being eyewitness on the Sun, we have grown to be the heart builders of the future Earthly-Human Sun, as free brothers and collaborators of Christ Himself.

The Earth being experienced its *Earthly-Human Sun-Birth.*

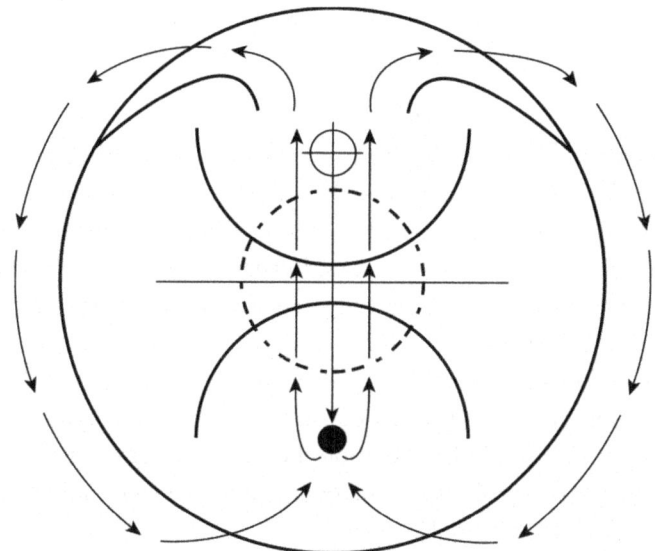

The Birth of the Earthly-Human Sun
(the arrows show the movement of the
turning inside-out of Shamballa)

4

The Relation Between Supersensible and Physical Events 1933-45

Here we shall add to the study of the occult significance of the 12 years 1933-45 a short indication concerning the special relation between the supersensible side of the Event and the main world events during these years. Research reveals an exact correlation between the two, but in such a way that everything positive above finds its opposite, an evil mirror-picture, on the Earth below. *Super*sensibly and *sub*physically: this was referred to in connection with the first stage of the Event, namely, with the picture of the divided Revelation. Let us now consider the main contrasts between the spiritual events and the *physical* events on the Earth during those 12 years.

Every historical study of the events on Earth at this time shows clearly that the centre of the Ego and Spirit-Self evolution of humanity falls wholly under the influence of the kingdom of evil—namely, the Bolshevistic USSR and Nazi Germany—precisely at the time when, in the supersensible world closest to the Earth, the Christ establishes His new Earthly-Human Sun Kingdom. Germany becomes the physical centre for the forces that directly fight against the true Ego evolution of humanity, and serves them with all its economic, social and cultural power.[47] For 12 years the Ego-centre of humanity is seduced and overpowered, possessed entirely by those demonic anti-Sun forces that separated, for this period of time, the true folk soul and spirit of the German people from their physical life and existence. And the development of their evil control clearly shows the evil mirror-picture of the three stages of the century's Imagination studied above.

---

[47] See K. Heyer, *Wesen und Wollen des Nationalsozialismus*, Perseus Verlag, 1992.

Let us briefly compare the supersensible and the physical events and place them over against each other.

At the beginning of the thirties the Revelation was taking place above, bringing to a certain culmination a process of preparation lasting two thousand years, since the Mystery of Golgotha. A new etheric earthly realm was created in which a seed group of Christ-permeated humanity will be spiritually and self-consciously active for the sake of humanity's future as a whole. On the Earth below the exact polar opposite takes place. Here also a kingdom is created and revealed, led by a seed group of human beings. But it is the kingdom in which the first self-conscious evil is systematically practised and developed as a basis for the whole future evil Ego evolution of humanity. Thus we have a new Earthly-Human Sun Kingdom above and a fully reversed, anti-human kingdom below: the new group of Christ-permeated humanity above, and the new group of the first fully-conscious servants of evil below. Above, freedom and love are practised for the first time as a self-conscious, creative, magical redeeming power; below, hatred is systematically developed as the future black art intent on the destruction and annihilation of the truly and uniquely human. A new spiritual, universal Michaelic 'race' is developed consciously above, by the small band of souls that remained loyal to Michael, while a new, subphysical, demonized race is produced below, in which human souls learn to suppress in themselves all individual human elements by means of special subhuman practices.

The 12 years are divided, first, into the six years of establishing and grounding the Earthly-Human Sun Kingdom above and the kingdom of evil below. In 1939 the true situation of humanity became a revealed fact. Then the war began, the first of its kind in human evolution so far. And then, precisely when the Michaelic drama was enacted above and the universal human question was formed and sacrificially realized, on the Earth below the opposite event took place. The war revealed its true form as the carefully planned destruction of the central human element. When the seed was prepared above for the future healing of humanity, below everything was done to achieve the greatest possible division of humanity into two wholly separated parts. When, seven years after 1933, in the year 1940/1, the 'final solution of the Jewish problem' was systematically put into action, and together with it the war was carried into Russia, that was the height of the decisive second phase. (Regarding the destruction of the past, present and future Ego evolution, as pointed out above, see note 43 to Chapter 3.) And when on the Earth the evil black art of annihilating the universally human was physically, self-consciously carried out in the age of the consciousness soul, from above, and reaching into the sub-earthly below, the greatest Manichaean sacrifice of Christ as the culmination of the second Mystery of Golgotha was taking place. It created 'at the same time' the human and divine archetype for the redemption of evil for all future ages to come. Precisely at the time when human beings—for the first time just because they *are* human beings, that is, carriers of the divine element in an earthly form—are physically destroyed, the Christ demonstrates, in the centre of human evil, the seed potential of the eternal union and oneness of all human beings in the being of God and in the heart of Christ-permeated Michaelic humanity.

The mirror-picture of the third stage is manifested exactly 'at the end' of the 12 years. At this time, as described above, the formerly divided Earth undergoes its Sun-Birth as a result of Christ's Sacrifice. It can now envelop and embrace its lowest being with its whole self, pouring out its life-giving Sun-power. It becomes a radiating etheric cosmic body, inwardly deeply wounded but health-giving and life-bestowing for its whole cosmic environment. Meanwhile, on the Earth below, the opposite, evil mirror-picture is created, bringing to expression an aspect of the specifically *Western* form of evil. The old cosmic Sun forces, materialized in the sub-earthly, demonized depths of matter are forcefully brought to the surface of the Earth as destructive, life-annihilating forces. The Atom bomb is created and exploded in 1945 as a means of annihilating human lives on a mass scale. This is the polar opposite of the gentle, upbuilding and healing Earthly-Human Sun-life stemming from the heart of the new Revelation and Sacrifice of Christ in His new etheric Kingdom.

5

The Rebirth of Anthroposophy since the End of the Twentieth Century

In his memoirs René Maikovski reports on an important conversation with Rudolf Steiner, in which the question concerning the number of potential anthroposophists in the world was discussed. After Rudolf Steiner made it clear that some millions of them exist, he added, noticing Maikovski's bewildered expression: 'The souls that seek Anthroposophy are incarnated; *but we don't speak their language!'*[48] Today, in the twenty-first century, after the catastrophic apocalyptic events of the twentieth century, only the smallest number of true Michaelic pupils are incarnated, who seek the path that leads to the new Michaelic movement. We must ask ourselves: Have we begun to speak the appropriate language of spiritual science, or is a considerable part of our anthroposophical life and thought straying behind the supersensible movement of our Time Spirit, Michael, and the true meaning of the new Christ Revelation?

If we look back at the 60s, we can see that only the peripheral seeds of the Christ Event could begin to incarnate. In the peripheral-external life of humanity they could find some suitable soil for their development, while the Michaelic mother-field remained infertile until the end of the century.

The first souls that carried these peripheral seeds to earth were born right at the close of the 12 years, and reached the age of 21 years in 1966/7. They were the first to lead the great social, ecological, political, cultural and spiritual transformations of the last third of the century. The first resurrected recurrence of the 12 years, which fell in the years 1967-79, was of great significance. The year 1966/7 brought to the unconscious *will* forces

---

[48] R. Maikovski, *Schicksalswege auf der Suche nach dem lebendigen Geist* (Verlag die Kommenden, Freiburg, 1980), p. 27.

of the young the first earthly tidings of the great Revelation of Christ's new Heaven and Earth. The year 1974/5 marks a significant, though hidden, moment. It began to bring to consciousness, individual heart perception of the first results of the crucial, central second stage of the century's Event, namely, Christ's Great Sacrifice. And the year 1979, which fell together with the completion of the first centennial Michael cycle, gave an inner *thought* impulse, as echo of the Sun-Birth of the Earth that rounded off the century's Event of the 12 years.

In this time, the central Michaelic impulse could begin to rise to consciousness on Earth, struggling in the deepening grave of civilization, to break through the hardening walls, that thickened more and more around the heart of humanity.

When we follow the development of this peripheral social-cultural stream, between 1966 and 1999, it is clear that even for the most creative people, that led the social and cultural changes, the real spiritual source of their inspiration remained unconscious. What is more, what they met as 'anthroposophy' in the external world, appealed very little to their creative and free spirits, and more often than not, they turned their spiritual search to other spiritual streams. One can estimate what a tremendous evolutionary force could have come about, if these people could have met a truly living Michaelic movement on Earth, in the centre of which the new Revelation of the Etheric Christ is actualized, that spoke to them in the universal-human language of the time. But the great majority of those who bore the century's Event in their unconscious will, feeling and thinking, and carried it into social and cultural life, could not find on Earth people that represented the mainstream of Michael and could not transform their unconscious forces into fully conscious spiritual activity. This meant that until the end of the century, only those who carried, unconsciously, the peripheral forces of the Spiritual Event, could work on Earth, while the true Michael School, in the etheric world, could not find acceptance on Earth. Those who realized the seeds of the Event in the periphery, were full of new, resurrected power and enthusiasm because it was inspired, unconsciously, by the supersensible Spiritual Event. But their way to a conscious grasp of the living stream of Michael was blocked. Only at the very end of the century it became possible, for the first time, to grasp it on Earth, and describe it in a fully conscious spiritual-scientific way, as we do here. At the end of the last century, this very narrow path had to be created, to bridge the deepening abyss, and cross over to this century, in which it can gradually develop.

It was part of the deeply shocking discoveries made in the 80s and 90s of last century, that from the greatly reduced Michael School in the etheric world, only a smallest part could incarnate towards the end of the century. This was caused by the tragic victory of the forces of hindrance in their fight against the Michael stream on the Earth in the twentieth century.

Our main task today is to communicate the spiritual-scientific research results of the direct connection that could be established with the developing Time Spirit and the Revelation of the Etheric Christ, through the investigation of the Spiritual Event of the twentieth century. The urgently needed bridge from the twentieth to the twenty-first centuries, across the abyss and grave of civilization has been built because we could resurrect the spiritual knowledge that Rudolf Steiner gave at the beginning of the century, and unite it with the presently active supersensible Michaelic stream. This narrow bridge, that has re-established a direct spiritual connection with the supersensible events of this century, must find a growing number of souls in the twenty-first century. This is possible since the end of the last century. This renewed possibility, that was realized as a result of the Spiritual Event of the twentieth century, is described in greater detail in the book, *The Twilight and Resurrection of Humanity: The History of the Michaelic Movement since the Death of Rudolf Steiner. An Esoteric Study.* There I show how the new Michaelic plan was created, to replace the original plan, that Rudolf Steiner described in 1924 in his lectures on the karma of the Michael stream. This cannot be dealt with here in greater detail, and we must refer the reader to this book.

The small band of Michaelic souls, that remained loyal to him through the Twilight of humanity and the apocalypse of the twentieth century, meet and recognized each other because they share the radical, revolutionary transformation of human soul faculties and the world's foundations that took place in the twentieth century. The Imagination of the century's Event described above is, in one way or another, a deeply-felt reality for them. They recognize one another through this fact. Their task today and in the first decades of the twenty-first century is to develop the new universal human language, and express the new stream of resurrected Christ-life, in a way that will be understood by all truly seeking souls.

The reopening of the spiritual world to conscious spiritual-scientific research is the esoteric aspect of the resurrection and rebirth of Anthroposophia at the end of the last century. The exoteric aspect must demonstrate this fact in the development of the Michael movement on Earth. This development is the main goal of the first part of this century. Into the grave of civilization the forces of resurrection are flowing from the supersensible Event of the century, in which the Michael stream played such a decisive role. It will bring forth its healing fruits in the first half of the twenty-first century. Out of the grave of modern civilization on all levels of human existence, the true spirit of the Michael-Christ Impulse will be resurrected, and become what it is destined to become for the Earth and for humanity in the consciousness soul age.

This will be possible when the *conscious*, earthly-human being Anthroposophia becomes a true eyewitness to the second Mystery of Golgotha, described above. Two thousand years ago this was the lot of the small band of souls assembled around Christ Jesus. They had participated in His life, death and resurrection. But to begin with, their conscious understanding of these mighty facts was rather limited. They could not yet comprehend the true nature of Christ's life and being, deeds and sacrifice. They went through the Mystery of Golgotha in a lowered state of consciousness. Peter denied the Christ early on Good Friday morning because he could not raise his consciousness to the level of the sacred events. Then, for 50 days, the disciples walked in Jerusalem as night wanderers, unconsciously united with the resurrected One, but yet unable to recognize Him in their daily consciousness. And then came the time of Pentecost. As Rudolf Steiner described it in his lectures on the Fifth Gospel,[49] the fire of the Holy Spirit awakened the disciples to the reality which they had already lived through. They were able to remember, to be aware and see the truth of Christ's life, death, resurrection and ascension.

And then they were able to bear witness to the reality that they had already experienced but only now could speak about. Fearlessly, they began to speak openly about the Mystery of Golgotha and the overcoming of death through Christ Jesus. They began to address the real mystery and riddle of their age, the riddle of death, and therefore they began to speak the universal human language of the heart, of the fourth post-Atlantean cultural epoch. And it is said[50] that all the peoples that represented humanity in Jerusalem understood them, because they spoke the true heart-language of humanity. In this way Christianity was founded and spread—from man to man, from heart to heart, 2000 years ago.

When we describe the Imagination of the century's Event, which is the renewing of the Mystery of Golgotha through evil, we become an eyewitness to the greatest Event of our fifth post-Atlantean cultural epoch. We were present in the etheric world when it occurred, as the disciples of Christ Jesus were present physically during His earthly life, death and resurrection. We were active participators in His renewed Revelation. The new Pentecost has verily been upon us since the 70s and 80s of this century. We stand now, at the end of the century, fully awakened, assembled around the appearance, words and deeds

---

[49] *The Fifth Gospel* (GA 148).
[50] Acts 2: 1-13.

of the resurrected Etheric Christ. We are now capable to describe, through the resurrected forces of modern spiritual science, what we experienced in the etheric world in this century. Then we can develop and speak, through the fire and light of the modern Pentecostal illumination of the end of the twentieth century, the universal human language of the heart, that expresses the spiritual mysteries of our age, in the form that is right for the age of the consciousness soul.

The Afterword to *The Twilight and Resurrection of Humanity*, 'The Resurrection of the Etheric Christ in the Twenty-first Century', ends with these prophetic words of Rudolf Steiner, spoken in 1910. This has indeed become, since the end of the century, 'the most momentous turning-point in the evolution of humanity' as he says, the new spiritual reality in which we live, weave and become:

> It is Christ who will lead men to His Shamballa [the etheric Earthly-Human Sun]... there will arise the experience of the land of the etheric Earthly-Human Sun, woven of light, shone through with light, teeming with wisdom. Such is the event which, for those who have the will to understand, for those who have ears to hear and eyes to see, must be described as denoting the most momentous turning-point in the evolution of humanity, through which men's understanding of the Christ Impulse will be enhanced and intensified... The more insight men achieve, the greater and mightier will Christ appear to them to be! When once their gaze can penetrate into the etheric Earthly-Human Sun... they will... grow into the realm where He will first be encountered: the mysterious land of the etheric Earthly-Human Sun.[51]

---

[51] See lecture of 6 March 1910 (GA 118).

Bibliography

Works by Rudolf Steiner referred to in the text and available in English translation (the latest editions are given):

GA	English title
1	*Nature's Open Secret*
2	*Goethe's Theory of Knowledge*
3	*Truth and Knowledge*
4	*The Philosophy of Freedom / Intuitive Thinking as a Spiritual Path*
9	*Theosophy*
13	*Occult Science*
18	*The Riddles of Philosophy*
20	*The Riddle of Man*
21	*The Riddles of the Soul*
26	*Anthroposophical Leading Thoughts*
35	*Philosophy and Anthroposophy* (forthcoming)
40	*Truth-Wrought-Words*
108	*Deeper Secrets of Human Evolution*
112	*The Gospel of St John and its Relation to the Other Gospels*
113	*The East in the Light of the West*
116	*The Christ Impulse and the Development of Ego Consciousness*
117	*The Deeper Secrets of Human Evolution in the Light of the Gospels*
118	*The Second Coming of Christ*
121	*The Mission of Folk-Souls*
123	*According to Matthew*
127	*The Mission of the New Spiritual Revelation*
130	*Esoteric Christianity*
133	*Earthly and Cosmic Man* (forthcoming)
143	*Three Paths to Christ*
148	*The Fifth Gospel*
152	*Approaching the Mystery of Golgotha*
176	*The Karma of Materialism*
180	*Ancient Myths and the New Isis Mystery*
185	*From Symptom to Reality in Modern History*
196	*What is Necessary in these Urgent Times*
200	*The New Spirituality and the Christ Experience of the Twentieth Century*
202	*Universal Spirituality and Human Physicality*
233a	*Rosicrucianism and Modern Initiation*

236   *Karmic Relationships, Vol. II*
237   *Karmic Relationships, Vol. III*
240   *Karmic Relationships, Vol. VI*
257   *Awakening to Community*
322   *The Boundaries of Natural Science*
326   *The Origins of Natural Science*
346   *The Book of Revelation and the Work of the Priest*

Titles are available from Rudolf Steiner Press, UK: www.rudolfsteiner-press.com and SteinerBooks, USA: www.steinerbooks.org

A note from the publisher

For more than a quarter of a century, **Temple Lodge Publishing** has made available new thought, ideas and research in the field of spiritual science.

Anthroposophy, as founded by Rudolf Steiner (1861-1925), is commonly known today through its practical applications, principally in education (Steiner-Waldorf schools) and agriculture (biodynamic food and wine). But behind this outer activity stands the core discipline of spiritual science, which continues to be developed and updated. True science can never be static and anthroposophy is living knowledge.

Our list features some of the best contemporary spiritual-scientific work available today, as well as introductory titles. So, visit us online at **www.templelodge.com** and join our emailing list for news on new titles.

If you feel like supporting our work, you can do so by buying our books or making a direct donation (we are a non-profit/charitable organisation).

office@templelodge.com

TEMPLE LODGE

For the finest books of Science and Spirit